On Wooden Wheels

On Wooden Wheels

the Memoir of Carla Nathans Schipper

Staccy Goldring

Copyright © 2005, 2006 by Stacey Goldring
Cover art credit: Renée Berg

Library of Congress Number:		2005904760
ISBN:	Hardcover	1-4134-9712-8
	Softcover	1-4134-9711-X

All rights reserved. No part of this book may be reproduced or transmitted in any form or by any means, electronic or mechanical, including photocopying, recording, or by any information storage and retrieval system, without permission in writing from the copyright owner.

This book was printed in the United States of America.

www.onwoodenwheels.com

To order additional copies of this book, contact:
Xlibris Corporation
1-888-795-4274
www.Xlibris.com
Orders@Xlibris.com
28927

CONTENTS

January 11, 2005	11
Born with Chicken Soup	22
June 2003	25
In the spiral	26
Solitary Musings	30
1930	44
Andre Andriesse	50
1938	55
1939	60
1940	63
1941	68
Not the Only One	70
1942	76
Behind a Funeral	79
With No Thought of the Future	84
Go Back to Bed	89
1943	97
The Offer	99
Collecting Fragments	114
Bernard Schipper	124
Hidden Years	145
A Fair Chance	155
Educating Jonathan	163
Laying a Foundation	170
Finding His Place	175
Filtered by Heart and Mind: Voices of the Daughters	197
From Snow to Sand	227

Acknowledgments	233
Notes	237
Glossary	241
Bibliography	249
Further Reading	251

Let my help come from the Lord, maker of Heaven and Earth.
—*Psalm 121*

Carla's life is woven like a long thick braid. Her relationships with people are closely bound, taking an intended twist, a purposeful turn. Through Carla's life, I've learned that she alone—barely reaching five feet tall, and eighty-seven years old—could bring the random chaos theory to an absolute grinding halt. Nothing is random in Carla's world. She is not one to pine over memories—horrible, nostalgic and sweet, or otherwise. Carla lives in the moment. She insists that her life, which spans experiences and years beyond the norm, is based on one simple concept: her belief in God. No matter how painful, unfair, or extraordinary her life may seem, Carla sees the meaning and richness in every memory. However, do not get any ideas of a woman with deep flowery philosophical expositions on her existence. No. What follows is exactly how Carla recalls her life. And let's put the emphasis on "exactly" right now. She is an intellectual with a penchant for numbers, dates, and places. Thanks to her husband Bernie, a researcher extraordinaire, if someone's identity is not recollected during one interview, you can take it to the bank that we will have that name the next time around. Carla's life is bound together with a profound belief in God, coupled with a highly philosophical view on life. This combination has yielded me a true friend and a vicarious experience in a not-so-distant time. I am forever grateful and unbelievably downright fortunate to record her story. How I wish that instead of this book, we could all be around Carla's dining room table, nibbling on candy and listening intently together.

Hopefully, this will suffice.

January 11, 2005

Armed with a stuffed dog, chocolate, and laptop, I set up shop in my usual spot: Carla's dining room table. Her son Jonathan is visiting his parents in Jacksonville, Florida. From New York, he comes down twice a year for ten days. That's the agreement that Carla and Bernie have with Bais Ezra, Jonathan's group home. I have never interviewed someone with Down syndrome. I am not sure what to expect. But you never know what to expect from an interview anyway.

I stopped by the chocolate shop beforehand and picked up a small plush dog and some chocolate-covered pretzels. I knew that Jonathan's birthday was coming up soon, so this would serve as an icebreaker. Chocolate knows no mental boundaries. It's a universal desire.

Jonathan was taking a nap. Carla told me that Jonathan was not in much of a good mood, but we would try the interview anyway. He was in bad spirits due to a quarrel he had with his counselor. She had spent the afternoon on the phone to the Bais Ezra in Brooklyn, trying to find out exactly what had happened. No one had straight answers. I could tell she had been down this road before. Although the person on the phone claimed to have no idea what Jonathan was talking about, Carla was sure that he was telling the truth. And like a repetitive dance move, Carla would take the forward steps of backing up Jonathan until the truth bowed in.

After a few minutes, Jonathan, forty-eight, emerges from the den. He looks sleepy. His kippah is on a little crooked, and Carla tells him to replace it on his head correctly. He does. Jonathan's features are a blend of his parents', translated by the softness of the Down tones. He is fair, stout, and has dark brown hair. His eyes are watery blue, like his father's. Jonathan's pants are belted high around his waist. His shirt is pressed, slightly wrinkled from his nap. Immediately I sense that he is testing me. His eye contact is, at first, minimal, but sharp. I remind myself of my objective. What exactly is it? Just follow wherever he leads.

I present my bad mood/peace offering/birthday gift. Jonathan pulls the dog from the purple bag, looks at it, and begins to stroke him gently. Jonathan's hand is as big as the dog. Why was I so cheap that I could not have gotten just a little bigger dog? A big smile broadens across his face. Jonathan reaches out toward me and plants a very large kiss on my cheek.

I'm in.

Next he examines the chocolate-covered pretzels. He holds the bag extremely close to his face. His movements are slow and deliberate.

"I know why you did this," he says.

"Because it's your birthday," I chime back.

"No. Because of Willy Wonka. Chocolate!" I glance at a color eight-by-ten framed photograph on the wall behind the stereo. I noticed it as soon as I came in. It is a new addition, I assume, a gift *from Jonathan on this visit. It's a great shot of him on stage, smiling, dressed in a tux, his arms outstretched, holding a cane and gold-sequined top hat: Willy Wonka. Jonathan was the lead. Carla and I had talked about his role in this theatrical production and his lead in many other plays organized by HASC, (Hebrew Academy for Special Children).*

"You are right," I tell him, more right than I realized.

"You made a good connection," he complimented.

"Thanks."

After this exchange, we settle into a silence. I then begin to ask some straightforward questions. Carla and Bernie are watching the news in the den. Reporters are blaring the obvious over and over about the recent tsunami disaster that has taken one hundred thousand lives. No, maybe more. Meanwhile, I dive, headfirst, into my own uncharted waters.

Q: Jonathan, tell me what you know about the Jewish people during World War II. [Is the question too complicated? Too condescending? I do not know.]

A: I was born after. I don't know that much.

Q: Do you know where your parents came from before New York?

A: She was born in Holland in Assen, and hubby was born in Germany. And his parents lived in Poland. And her parents were born in Assen.

Q: Do you know how your parents met?

A: In Holland.

Let me explain right here that the interview, on paper, looks, so far, pretty smooth and very tidy.

It's not.

Jonathan takes very long pauses. He stutters. He looks down. He breathes heavily. Each of these strenuous pauses fills me with apprehension. In other words, I begin sweating profusely. Carla has cautioned me that Jonathan can become easily frustrated when people do not understand him. I do not want to go down that road.

Q: Do you know about the Holocaust?

A: Used to. Well, you can say, used to have these so-called nightmares.

Q: What were they?

A: [Jonathan intently studies the little stuffed dog. It's a dwarf cocker spaniel.] She. They. When they used to have company, used, they used to talk about it.

I invoke executive decision upon myself. Under any other circumstances, I certainly would probe deeper, never accepting "they" and moving on. "Who are 'they'?" or "To whom are you exactly referring when you say 'they'?" But I am in unfamiliar territory, and it is already late in the afternoon. I go with my gut instinct. "They" must mean his parents, Carla and Bernie. Maybe this is a grave error. I push on.

Q: What did they say?

A. [Jonathan strokes the little dog's ear.] Used to. [He squeezes his eyes shut in concentration.] Used to. Sleeping.

Q: Did you hear what they said? Can you tell me what they said?

A: Concentration camps. I was not born yet. I was born with the German Jews. Yankee.

Q: What do you mean by "Yankee"? Who is Yankee? Your uncle? [Carla's son-in-law goes by the nickname Yankee. It is short for Yaakov.]

A: That means you have to be on time to go to shul to daven. And this counselor I knew at home. I was not ready on time. I cussed him out.

He has changed the subject. Why? I do not know. But I'm following now. I suppose he is still upset about the quarrel.

Q: Did you solve the problem?

A: The house manager, Monte, helped solve the problem.

Case closed. I lead now.

Q: Do you remember your bar mitzvah, Jonathan?

A: [He looks around for a picture, some reference. Carla's bookshelves are filled with framed photographs of family.] Yeah.

Q: What was your portion?

A: *Pinchas.* [He smiles at the *clickety-click* sound of my typing and gives my laptop screen the once-over.] That's spelled P-I-N-C-H-U-S!

Q: Tell me about being Jewish, Jonathan. [Why do I keep saying his name? Am I condescending to him, trying to keep his attention? What?] Is it important to you?

A: Oh yeah. My family. Like, you see, all my nieces. [Jonathan points to the bookcase.]

Q: Is this part of being Jewish, all these people?

A: And part of the Goldstein clan got married—that guy with the glasses. [He points to a bride-and-groom photo, by his Willy Wonka photo.] I can't see him anymore.

Q: Who?

A: My nephew [the groom].

Q: Jonathan, do you know that your mother hid during the Holocaust and saved her life that way?

A: Yeah. Did she tell you that she became a nurse?

Q: Yes, she told all about becoming a nurse. Did she tell you anything else about herself when she was younger?

A: No. Only hubby! Study.

Q: Who studied?

A: Hubby with his brother in a shul in Frankfurt. And guess what I had for lunch? Frank-furt-ers! And coleslaw and cake!

Puns! I love puns. I burst out laughing. He does too.

"Is it possible, instead of having you write," he says, *"would you like to be my first guest for my birthday? If you bring your hubby, after Shabbos? If you are married—you are, aren't you?"*

"Yes, I am," I tell him. *"My hubby's name is Bruce."*

"Like Bruce Springsteen! All right!" [Jonathan begins to "jam" on his air guitar.]

Q: Do you remember growing up in Washington Heights?

A: That was before I had the pills. And group homes.

Jonathan begins to quiet down. I need to get moving.

Q: Do you have good memories about going to Camp Ramah? [Jonathan attended sleep-away camp for seven summers in Palmer, Massachusetts.]

A: She was there, and she decided to come here, Gail, my nurse. She [Carla] didn't tell you?

"Jonathan, that's how your mom and I met. Gail, your nurse at camp, is my cousin, and she introduced me to your mother! Isn't it a small world?"

"Ahhhhhh . . . That's a small world." He smiles.

Q: What else do you remember from camp?

A: Daven.

Q: What else?

A: Eat, of course.

Q: Did you have fun?

A: Yeah.

Q: Do you have fun now, Jonathan?

Nothing from him. He is completely quiet.

Q: What have people told you about World War II?

A: That guy, he killed my whole family, Adolf Hitler. And he, that guy, and the other guy. This young guy, in *The Sound of Music*, he wants to become a trained Nazi.

Q: What was his name? Rudolf. Rudy?

A: Rolf.

Q: That's it.

A: That's the one. [In the movie] the captain says to him, "Don't be like them, boy. Stay with us." "Intruders!" Rolf yells.

Q: Do you remember other movies about World War II?

A: Austria.

Q: Do you remember what your parents would talk about when they would talk about the camps with the company?

A: Twisting and turning.

Q: You were in your bed listening to your parents? Is this why you were twisting and turning? Was it upsetting to you?

A: Yes. [Here again, Jonathan disconnects with me. I am now comfortable about the silence, although I am well aware that it is dinnertime. Carla has peeked out once already. Where is she now? I could use a little help.] She. I told her. Why I was born Down syndrome?

Q: What did she say?

A: It's a gene. I was born with a gene, and it was in the center of my brain.

Q: Did your parents think you were sleeping when they had company over?

A: I was watching from my room.

Q: Did you ever talk to your sisters about it?

A: No.

Q: Why?

A: [Shrugged shoulders]

Q: Do you remember going to Israel?

A: For plastic surgery. Boy, that was a tough one to beat. Pain. And lots of it. It makes me sleepy. Too much anesthesia makes me dizzy sometimes. [Jonathan points to his cheekbones, tongue, and chin, indicating where he had plastic surgery.] Here. Here and here.

Q: Are you glad you had the plastic surgery?

A: I guess so, yeah.

Now Jonathan asks me a question.

Q: Is it possible when it comes out, in paper?

A: Do you want a copy?

Q: Yeah. I like to have, soft.

A: You mean a paperback?

Q: Yeah.

A: Sure, I can give you a soft one.

**

1866

> English physician John L. H. Langdon-Down first recognizes the syndrome, termed Down syndrome, identifying fewer than a dozen characteristics.

Up until the 1960s

> Most doctors recommend that parents place their Down-syndrome child in an institution. It is believed that this course of action is best for the family and the child. Much of this belief rests upon the assumption that the problems of the condition are biological, and that environmental aspects have little influence, so that there is no reason to try to stimulate or teach children with Down syndrome.

1950s to 1960s

Addressing Down syndrome facial characteristics and plastic surgery, a large number of studies are conducted that investigates the relationship between the physical characteristics of people with Down syndrome and level of ability. None can be found.[1]

1959

Jerome Lejeune and Patricia Jacobs, researchers working independently, first determine that the cause of Down syndrome is, trisomy,[2] *triplication of the twenty-first chromosome.*

1960s to 1970s

Several research studies compare the mental and social development of children who live and are cared for at home, or fostered with a family, with the development of those who live in institutions. Those children living at home are usually found to be more developmentally advanced, to have more outgoing behavior, and to have acquired a larger range of interests and social skills.

Before 1978

Most children with Down syndrome in the United States attend institutions or segregated schools because they are considered to be uneducable and unable to benefit from education.[3]

※ ※

Born with Chicken Soup

"I don't think I was too happy about being pregnant with Jonathan," Carla admits. "It was a little after a Seder that I found out I was pregnant. You know, you have a little wine . . . I wasn't always so well anyways. I always had problems with my intestines. And sometimes you do not feel so good. So I missed a period, but didn't think it was a big deal. We were living here in the United States already."

Carla does not recall anything peculiar about her pregnancy with Jonathan; she only remembers that she was low in folic acid. "My body wasn't making it. It has become apparent, today, that this may be responsible for the retardation."

With a steady rhythm of words, Carla recalls Jonathan's birth and her experience shortly thereafter:

> On January 15, 1957, Tuesday, my son Jonathan was born. I gave birth at Fifth Avenue Hospital. It was very elegant in those years. I had a hard time giving birth, but of course, I made it. Bernie was elated that it was a boy. He came to my room and sat next to my bed. I "came to" on Wednesday, but they didn't let

me see much of Jonathan. But when they brought him to me, I saw something on him. You have to realize I worked in a psychiatric hospital in Holland. I recognized something on him. There was something wrong. That was the reason they didn't bring him to me right away. Monday, the regular doctor came to my room and said that the head of pediatrics wanted to talk with me. On Tuesday, he came with a couple of nurses. They said that they weren't sure of his development. They did not use the words "Down syndrome." But there were signs that it didn't have to be that way. Naturally, we didn't want this. But they were not lying to us. They thought that he might be [Down syndrome], but they also knew of kids like Jonathan that had normal development and they did not know how his development would be. That was the end of the discussion.

The Schippers went home with their newborn son by taxi. They did not say anything about their concerns about Jonathan to their daughters, Channa, eighteen, Jedidjah, fifteen, and Ruthie, nine. "We didn't know ourselves," Carla states.

Once settled in at home, like all Jewish newborn boys, Jonathan's bris was performed eight days after his birth. After a few weeks, Jonathan had his first visit with a pediatrician. Carla clearly recalls the conversation she had with the doctor. The doctor, a Hungarian Jewish woman. She told the Schippers that they had to give Jonathan away. "I asked her," Carla says, "What are you talking about?"

Carla left, aghast, absolutely furious at the suggestion that Jonathan be institutionalized. However, this doctor also told Carla to try to feed Jonathan chicken bouillon with a spoon. "It saved his life," she says. What kind of baby was Jonathan? Did he look or behave differently than other infants? Was he a Down-syndrome child? Perhaps he was a borderline case or something else entirely. Carla's instinct told her that he was different. What that difference was, she did not know. She knew that Jonathan could not drink from a bottle properly. In Down-syndrome infants, this is usually due to the immaturity and weakness of the sucking and swallowing reflexes and muscles.[4] Instead, she fed him chicken broth with a spoon. Today, Jonathan will tell people that he was born with chicken soup. "We were always contemplating, was he or wasn't he? You have to realize what we went through not knowing. This 'not knowing' went on for a very long time."

In 1958, several tests revealed that Jonathan, almost two years old, was a "borderline case." He had no signs of abnormality in his brain and hips, which Carla explains are markers for the syndrome. However, his fingerprints and lines on his hands were straight, whereas normal genetics would lead to swirl-shaped fingerprints. Although diagnosed with this semi-Down status, Carla still saw an exceptional instinct in her son. She was determined to seek out the best care for her child. In addition, she and her husband were also committed to raising their son as an Orthodox Jew. Dealt the colossal task of creating an enriching life for a child that, at the time, American society would simply institutionalize and ignore, Carla was also carrying the weight of her past.

June 2003

During my first visit with Carla, we chatted for a while—me, seated on her sofa, and she in one of her Danish teak dining room chairs. Our talk was exploratory and guarded. Carla was sizing me up, and I her. Was I the right person to chronicle her thoughts and experiences? Was she someone I could connect to and understand? Was she serious about this idea? Was I? As we interviewed each other, she revealed that she had already written "a little something." I asked to see it. Carla left the room and promptly returned with a small thin spiral notebook. She stood in front of her chair and, as if delivering a classroom book report, began to read.

Carla's rhythmic writing style and use of language was befitting of a proper Dutch upbringing. She was articulate in her oration and thorough in her story's detail. When she finished, ending with her parents' early-married life, I asked to see her notes. She handed me the small spiral. Her handwriting was neat, uniform, and single-spaced. No mistakes. I asked if it would be okay if I could possibly transcribe the notes to use later.

I committed.

She agreed.

I left the interview with her spiral, her first of her many gifts to me.

In the spiral

A child was born to Joseph Hirsch and Johanna Francisca Hartog-Nathans. The date was August 13, 1917, in Groningen. My mother, Johanna, thirty-nine years old, was not young anymore when she got married, and gave birth after being married for nine years. She came from a very well to do family in Waalwyk N. Brabant, the middle child of three: Louise, her sister, and Leon her younger brother.

Johanna had received a very good education in a finishing school in Frankfurt am Main and Wiesbaden, Germany.

My father, Joseph, came from a family in Assen, the capital of the province Drente. The family had seven children: six boys and one girl. Joseph Nathans's father was a well-to-do businessman. From his six sons, he sent four to university to become doctors and a lawyer, and my father went originally to the Jewish Seminary in Amsterdam in order to become a rabbi. However, that left only one son to take over the family business. Since this son was a lilliput, my father was called back from his studies to come into the business with my grandfather.

My father's return to take over the family business happened about approximately fifteen years before I was born. As was customary in those years, families sought to arrange for good marriages. It was important to find financially well-off families in which to marry. My grandfather went especially out of his way to find proper wives for his sons. How the connection with my mother's family was exactly made, I never heard. I only was told that my grandmother right away fell in love with my father! My highly sophisticated and refined mother had to leave her birthplace in the south and go to live in the northern part of Holland; in those years, the distance was vast.

She had to adjust to a totally different environment from where she came. Johanna entered a lively household, where my grandmother ruled with a scepter and my grandfather was a fun-loving but respected gentleman and businessman. My father was a very outgoing individual, while my mother was reticent and introverted.

Dressed chic, according to her style, she came for the first time to make her acquaintance with the family. As the anecdote goes, my grandmother told her that she was wearing would only be worn in "Assen, by the wife of the mayor." That must have been some welcome for my poor (nice) mother.

The first years of their marriage were good. My father had many friends. They held Jewish study programs, called *shiorim*. And they were sociable, although for my mother it was not easy to find someone with whom she had anything in common. They were a little bit on the upper outside. For instance, most of the people that lived in Assen were farmers. My mother was much more sophisticated. She didn't have a chance to express this or get close to anybody. Her mother, Kaatje Hartog, lived with my parents for a while. She had ALS or something, I don't know for sure. My parents had a nurse to take care of her. In those years, my parents were well to do, but in 1929 or 1930 it became tricky. In 1929, things got pretty bad in business [due to the onset of the world-wide Great Depression] but my father was able to sustain. I never knew Kaatje Hartog or my grandfather. Johanna and Joseph Nathans found that starting a family was a very painful endeavor. My mother had several miscarriages. My uncle, a physician, came once to visit my parents around 1916. He lived in The Hague and had a huge practice that was favored throughout the community.

He told my mother to come to a clinic in The Hague, where doctors could probably help her with her gynecological problems. She took his advice. After practically a decade of failed pregnancies, I was born in a hospital in Groningen, a half-hour train ride from Assen, where another uncle lived who was also a physician.

In those years, it must again have been quite an ordeal for my mother to go through because most women gave birth in the home, as opposed to going into the hospital. All this information I found out through my girlfriends. My mother never told me these things.

So now, they had a little girl who was to be their only child. My father was delighted. I do not know how my mother felt about me or how she was able to take care of me. She was a sickly, delicate person.

Over the next two years, our interviews took place at Carla's. She and her husband, Bernie, live at The Coves, a Jewish retirement community in Jacksonville, Florida. The campus is understated and calm, surrounded by trees. One-story homes with simple architectural details attach to River Garden, the city's Jewish Retirement home. Each small home has its own front door. Carla's front entrance is particularly inviting, with climbing deep purple bougainvillea thriving around her petite portico. Roses, a fig tree, potted plants and herbs sit on the patio. Mums, hydrangeas, and other flowers sit in the corner garden. These are Bernie's charges.

Perched in a row on the front windowsill sit six healthy small African violets. The aesthetic quality is important to Carla. Living in a Jewish environment is a necessity. Carla and Bernie get most of their meals "to go" in white Styrofoam boxes from the main dining room. Carla cannot cook anymore like she used to. Through their home's interior back door and down a hallway, Carla and Bernie have access to meals, lectures, library, swimming pool, dining room, religious and medical services—a general sense of community.

Inside Carla's home, our conversations took place at her dining room table. On her linen floral tablecloth covered with a clear plastic always sat hard candies and chocolates for us to nibble, and chilled water for me to drink. Depending on the time of year, a variety of flowers in a small vase graced our spot. We established a routine early on: Carla always sat in her usual place, the chair layered with a few seat cushions, situated closest to the kitchen. I sat always caddy corner to her. She would sip her tea, answer my questions, use the bathroom and apologize for having to use the bathroom. Her home is serene. It is absolutely incomprehensible for me to fully understand how her past could be filled with immense horror and dread when presently, all is so calm.

Solitary Musings

*T*he earliest documented presence of Jews in the Netherlands dates from the twelfth century when Spanish Jews fled Spain's Inquisition and settled in the Netherlands. By the mid-1500s, the Jewish community was expelled or destroyed.

Late 1500s

> Portuguese Marranos, Jews forcibly converted to Christianity who remained secret Jews, and descendants of Portuguese Marranos living in Belgium and Italy began to settle in the Netherlands and practiced Judaism openly.[5] This group settled in an area adjacent to what is now the Jonas Daniel Meijerplein. They were the first generation of the Jewish community that was to endure until the German occupation.

Early 1600s

> In the 1620s, a second group of Jews immigrated to the Netherlands. The new arrivals from Germany formed a

semiautonomous Ashkenazic "nation." Their Polish and Lithuanian coreligionists fleeing from pogroms in Ukraine joined these German Jews three decades later. The two groups together were known as the Hoogduitse, "High German," nation. With a population of five thousand in 1680, and thirty thousand a century later, theirs was a far larger community than that of their Sephardic cousins. It was also much poorer.[6] By and large, these Jews enjoyed tolerance and security in the Netherlands; and after the founding of the Batavian Republic in 1795, Jews were granted complete emancipation.[7]

1800s to 1900s

Dutch anti-Semitism was directed mainly against the Hoogduitse, perhaps because the Portuguese Jews were seen as an exotic community with a glorious past. The Sephardic Jews' very reason for being in the Netherlands fit the Dutch conception of its own struggle against Spain. They were, in essence, fellow sufferers. Dutch anti-Semitism was not seen as dangerous, but as a slightly unpleasant element in an otherwise safe, if impoverished, existence.[8]

**

I was named Carla. I was supposed to be named Kaatje after my grandmother on my mother's side. My parents didn't like that name. Carla was an unusual name for that time. I was aware that I was pestered, but I didn't know why. As a child, I took it all in stride.

Carla's childhood memories extended far back and clearly to 1923 at the age of six, when she started school. Her experience was rather melancholy with no close friends. She does remember in the third or fourth grade having one little girlfriend named Corrie.

> The first school year was all right. There was even a boy in the class, who told me that he wanted to marry me after he was grown up. But for some reasons, which I never understood, the children in the other classes teased and called me names. Although I was a very good student, I could not comprehend why they did that to me. Later, I thought it was because I looked a little Chinese or Japanese because my eyes were a little slanted. Also, my clothes were not especially the same as the other children. Apparently, my mother did not know or pay attention to what other kids were wearing.

And then, very slowly, Carla became friendly with two very particular girls who would become an integral thread in the framework of her rich life: Leida van Tyn and Tetta Hazekamp.

> Leida's father worked for cattle dealers, and her mother was a nice woman. Leida was very smart and well loved because she had nice blonde curly hair. As young kids, we went with boys. We would talk after school, riding our bikes or stand in the street. My close girlfriend, Tetta, told to me that I was not dressed properly. But my mother was too old for me. My mother went with me to an old dressmaker, a woman who never married, to have my clothes made. My mother was very nice; don't misunderstand me. I knew that she was different. It was obvious to me that she just didn't belong in Assen. She came from a totally different family and environment, and it's not easy.

Tetta Hazekamp became Carla's closest friend. She was not Jewish. Her family was not sophisticated, although Carla remembers that Tetta's father had a passion for William Shakespeare. "He knew Shakespeare from A to Z. Such things can bring you, in a way, to another planet. Tetta's mother was nice. They were very nice people, gentle, *haimish*," Carla fondly recalls.

> When I first met Tetta and Leida, I saw that they were dressed very neat and pretty—just regular dresses which their mothers made for them. I told my mother that from now on I wanted to choose my own clothing, meaning that the seamstress could still make them for me, but I wanted her to make things that I liked! Unknowingly, that really helped somehow my self-esteem. Subsequently, I got closer to my two friends Leida and Tetta. At a certain time after we were already quite close, I suggested that we form a friendship club with a real name, the TECALEI Club: the TE from Tetta, the CA for Carla, and LEI from Leida.

Once a week, the members of TECALEI would gather in the evening at Carla's house, primarily because out of the three Carla was the only one who had her own room. Privacy was a priority for the young girls' club.

A successful club needs members and capital. The girls decided to ask the TECALEI parents to join, in absentia, and donate ten cents every week for entertainment purposes. Before each meeting started, after they collected their membership money, and along with their spare pocket money, they went off to the candy store to buy something for their weekly evening get-togethers.

> It was serious business. Leida was the treasurer, and I the president. We wrote the minutes—I think that

was Tetta, she was the secretary. The minutes were very important, of course. They contained all the information of the previous week. For instance, which boy had paid attention to one of us, or who was going with whom. Do not forget here that we were aspiring teenagers. The most important subject, of course, was the other sex. During the meeting we noshed from the stuff we had bought. Sometimes my mother wanted to know if we needed something to drink, but mostly she left us alone, laughing and giggling.

The club existed at least a year or a little more. Then, once the girls started preparing for high school, the weekly TECALEI meetings tapered off.

Carla attended the Assen gymnasium (high school). Students could choose from two different high school tracks: HBS (Hogere Burger School) or gymnasium. "The more sophisticated and well-off families steered their children towards gymnasium." These schools differed in subject matter. The HBS was for students who were more interested in math and sciences. The gymnasium taught Latin, Greek, English, French, and German. Leida went to the HBS. In 1932, Tetta and Carla were accepted to attend the gymnasium in Assen.

Like the majority of those in Holland, Tetta and Carla rode their bicycles to school.

The environment at the gymnasium allowed Carla to find her own self. Carla's feelings of inadequacies as a young child and transformation as a teenager were kept private. She did not discuss these feelings with her mother or father, although she may have shared these thoughts with Tetta's mother. "My parents were not bad. They just did not know how to deal with me."

> I went there four years and blossomed out. Was it because of being dressed better or the self-esteem

within me? It was something that people have in their makeup from birth. I always thought that I didn't belong, but slowly, people started to recognize me. When they asked me to be on the student council, this was something I never would have dreamt of. This was a revelation. When you are on the student council, you are invited to attend meetings and go to parties. It was a good experience. It was such a nice part of my life. I had my own room at home, and I'd study with boys, together. It was all so innocent. It sounds so crazy now. Who would do that nowadays? There was nothing bad about it. It was just like your girlfriends.

Carla and Tetta were very close and shared their most personal thoughts. Tetta commented that Carla's father was never nice to her mother. Carla was already keenly aware of her parents' coolness and not at all offended when Tetta shared this very personal observation. "I remember going to the train station to meet Carla's father," Tetta wrote recently in a letter to Carla. "We'd be playing, and Carla's mother would come find her and tell her that they had to go to the train station to greet her father, who would travel weekly to the bourse [stock market]. It was expected of them to be there, waiting for him when he got off the train. I'd come along with Carla and her mother. I remember that he'd get off the train and walk right by them. He barely greeted us. He paid little attention to Carla. She was a fixture, just there. It didn't even affect her after a while. He always made such a big ceremony, insisting that they be there. I never understood it."

Tetta Hazenkamp, as a child, was constantly reminded of the Nathanses' awkward family dynamics. She recalls, "Carla's father was a strange man. They didn't have a good marriage. Carla's mother was a lovely woman, but she couldn't show it. She lived in her own world."

In contrast, Tetta's home served as a warm, comforting haven for Carla. "When I would come from school, I'd drop off my bags and head to Tetta's. There, Tetta's mom was waiting with tea and cookies! We'd chat and have good mother-daughter talks."

During summer vacations, Carla was sent to southern Holland. There she spent precious times with her maternal aunt Louise Hartog, who she affectionately describes as "a refined lady who was deaf." Carla's summer experiences with her cosmopolitan aunt had a great influence on her life.

Her distant father, Joseph Nathans, was involved in local politics. He was a well-respected Democrat and was elected to the Assen City Council. Carla recalls that once, in his capacity as a councilman, he attended a luncheon in a palace of then Queen Juliana, and received a kosher meal.

Joseph Nathans embraced new inventions. Their home, on the stately Noordersingel Street in Assen, had a central heating system installed throughout for Carla's mother's health. Carla's father felt a constant temperature in every room of their home, as opposed to just select rooms, would alleviate his wife's battles with asthma and bronchitis. In the early 1920s, this was a very modern way of heating a home.

Although Carla's father, Joseph, made accommodation for his wife's health and comfort, Johanna was never at ease with her lifestyle as a wife and mother in Assen. Johanna never outwardly shared her unhappiness with Carla. However, Carla knew that her mother's background contrasted sharply with the life in which she was consigned.

She remembers her mother as quiet and subdued. Johanna was six years older than Carla's father. Her family came from the village Waalwijk, in southern Holland. Johanna was educated in refined German finishing schools.

Few stories of her family background ever seeped into Carla's collective family history. She does know that Johanna's mother, the matriarch, stayed at home and ran a store that sold farming materials.

Like any Jewish community, the Dutch Waalwijk Jewish community had its share of differing points of view. Carla recalls a story her mother did share about the shul's members' differing opinions, in which her grandfather ultimately had the final word: "My grandfather walked out with the Sefer Torah in his hands and started davening someplace else," laughs Carla.

"In Assen, my mother didn't have many friends because the Jewish people of that town were not very sophisticated people, let's put it that way. My mother could speak French and German. I do remember that she had a close friend from England. So her friends were more learned and sophisticated women. This didn't exist in Assen, where I came from."

Johanna's formal cosmopolitan upbringing and fine tastes withered in the country life. Johanna wanted to be a member of WIZO (Women's International Zionist Organization), but Joseph was against it. As a strict Orthodox Jew, he rejected Zionism. This clash left a rift in the marriage because Johanna went to the meetings anyway. "She was ahead of her time," observes Carla.

Joanna was always busy, attending meetings, reading, doing fine crocheting and needlework. "But she would not make a dress."

Although Johanna was brought up as an Orthodox Jew, she was not as observant as her husband Joseph. He studied to become a rabbi in Amsterdam at the Orthodox Seminary. His studies were all encompassing and rigorous.

During the high holidays of Rosh Hashanah and Yom Kippur, smaller Dutch Jewish communities would be in need of a *hazzan* to lead services. Not for pay, only room and board, Carla's father accepted these positions year after year, traveling to the small towns of Rijssen and Meppel with Carla and Johanna in tow. This was his calling, and subsequently, their duty.

Carla's mother came from a family that kept Shabbat and kosher... "and that's about it. My father would daven and lay tefillin, and in the evening, go to minyan. It was done just because his parents did it that way and everybody does it that way. But my mother followed because she *had to*. For instance, if we were *bensching*, she'd say, 'I don't know what I am saying.' My father would say, 'Okay, it doesn't matter.' That was the nature of their relationship. This disregard for my mother's intellect bothered me, even at the age of twelve."

Carla had all the trappings of a well-to-do young girl. She was given piano lessons. She had her very own room and lived in a beautiful home. But all these accoutrements garnered no warm fondness. Her father's proclivity toward coldness is etched in Carla's memory.

> I can see my father sitting at his desk doing paperwork, writing a postcard, and my mother was busy doing something as well. For Shabbos, my father would send a postcard to his brother in The Hague or to my aunt in Utrecht. Just a little schmooze and mail it so they had something for Shabbos. I don't know how the mail worked. Maybe he'd send on a Thursday. It was a very nice gesture. But anyway, he'd say, "Johanna, would you get a postcard for me." She'd have to drop everything to get that card for him. This infuriated me. I couldn't stand that my father treated my mother in such a way.

Joseph Nathans's warehouse manager used to come to Carla's home and visit with her father on Fridays before Shabbat. Carla recalls that her father would call her mother into the room and say something like, "Is that a new dress? Turn around and show me." This incensed Carla. "To say that, in front of the employee. It made me so angry. Even at a young age I realized that he was treating her poorly."

Carla's relationship with both her mother and father had an awkward bent; she was like an extra appendage which neither Joseph nor Johanna could understand how to use.

> For instance, when I was ten or eleven at that time, doll carriages were fashionable. They were really beautiful and made to look authentically like the real ones. They were built low and were enclosed. I used to love them. I hoped I would get one. I didn't. It wasn't because we were poor. We were not. It was because I was an only child, and they didn't want to spoil me. Instead, my father picked up an old-fashioned doll carriage with iron wheels and rattan and gave it to me. I was ashamed to go outside. I had to go with that in the street, with the children and with the other carriages. If you have ten children, okay. For my father, that was good enough for me. I never forgave him for that. A couple of years later by the time I was eleven or twelve, I had a birthday. And they didn't get anything for me.

Carla pauses.

> No one said anything the whole day. I still see my father, in front of his desk. I said, "You couldn't get me something for my birthday?" He said, "What do you want?" I said, "A book. Just something." I watched him. He picked up the phone and called the most expensive bookstore in Assen and ordered two books that were the most not connected to a young girl. One had something to do with the exploration of the North or South Pole. I don't even know if my mother said to my father, "Give her something." In those years, they started Mother's Day. I was about nine, and I heard about it. And I said, Okay, I want to buy something for

> my mother. I bought a bag, a shopping bag, and gave it to her. It was striped, rather casual. I could tell she didn't like it. It was green and black with a handle. So I could tell she was disappointed.

In 1929, during the Depression, Joseph Nathans looked for extra income. While reading the Jewish newspaper, *Niew Israelitisch Weekblad*, he saw a want ad from a couple seeking a good temporary Jewish household for their young Jewish children. The couple was in divorce proceedings and needed foster care.

> My father discussed the probability of having to take care of two young children with my mother. This was a huge responsibility for my mother. But of course, she gave in and took the children! Here is my mother, a sickly lady, and I am thirteen. The children are four and six years old and coming from Amsterdam. We are in a small city. At the least, it was a totally different atmosphere, and here comes the two wild kids. I was mad at my father. My mother was sick. The kids made fun of her. After these children were with us for a couple of weeks, their father and brother-in-law came to visit. Originally, the kids were not supposed to see the parents. The mother was supposedly an unstable individual. But somehow an agreement about visitation was reached, and the father and his brother-in-law visited frequently.

Carla's parents struck up a close relationship with the brother-in-law, the sophisticated Mr. —— Mendelson. He wanted to reciprocate Johanna and Joseph Nathans's generosity for having his niece and nephew in their home. Carla was to be the happy recipient of the adults' agreement.

The Mendelsons of Amsterdam had three children: Emil, eleven, and two younger children whose names Carla does not recall. Carla, fourteen years old in 1931, began to spend time in Amsterdam with this warm and loving family. She particularly enjoyed the brotherly bond she shared with Emil.

> They treated me like a princess. It was like another part of my life. Mrs. Mendelson was somewhere between a mother and a sister to me. I didn't have that relationship with my mother. They took me all over Amsterdam. This beautiful experience with this family was like a revelation for me. My father was on the go, and my mother was not available to me. This family, with its warmth, was so new and pleasant.

However aloof the parenting, Carla and her father shared a common bond in their devotion to Judaism.

For Carla, growing up in Holland, girls completed their Torah studies at age twelve and then focused on a life of domesticity.

Not Carla.

She wanted more. Carla's father did too. His desire was to become a rabbi. This dedication to their faith ran deep throughout the Nathanses' family history.

Joseph Nathans's grandfather, Carla's paternal great-grandfather, Meier Joune Hirsch, was also a rabbi. According to Carla, in 1745, the *Opperrabijn*, the head rabbi of Holland, instituted a program of language assimilation for the large number of Jews who were fleeing the pogroms of Eastern Europe and seeking refuge in the Netherlands. Instead of this new Dutch-Jewish population learning Hebrew and speaking Yiddish, they were to learn Hebrew and speak Dutch. Rabbi Meier Joune Hirsch, a very prominent Dutch-Jewish scholar, was responsible for implementing this edict. As a result, during those years, no Dutch Jews used Yiddish.

Consequently, no children learned Yiddish. In Carla's house, no Yiddish was ever spoken. Any Yiddish language Carla subsequently picked up she learned in America.

Joseph Nathans's commitment to Judaism would not take the same path as his grandfather. Although he had five brothers—Leezer, Samuel, Abraham, Herman, William—and a sister, Reina, it was he who his father, Moses Nathans, ultimately tapped to carry on the family's metal and rags business, Lompen en Metalen. Sometime during 1903, Joseph Nathans left his rabbinical studies at the Jewish Theological Seminary in Amsterdam and returned to Assen to take over the business.

As a businessman, Joseph Nathans was a leader in Assen's Orthodox Jewish community, which numbered approximately one hundred fifty. As a father, he personally taught Carla to read Hebrew. "I didn't go to Hebrew school. The teachers, two elderly men, couldn't discipline the students nor teach very well. My father felt they were inadequate, and they didn't keep the level of observance that my father demanded. We were strictly Orthodox. However, when my father became a member of the school board, then I had to go to Hebrew school," Carla explains. After that traditional Hebrew school education ended, Carla wanted to learn more. She urged her traditional father to find a teacher for her. Her father eventually relented to her determination to continue her Jewish studies, securing the hazzan of Assen to teach Carla. Joseph Nathans and the hazzan arranged for Carla to be privately tutored in the hazzan's home. The hazzan's daughter, two years younger, sat in on his lessons with Carla as well. He accepted no fee. The avant-garde arrangement worked well. Carla was able to immerse herself in Judaism and was on the path to becoming a certified Jewish Studies teacher.

Whereas Joseph Nathans embraced Judaism's practice, prayers and rituals, Carla delved deeper, forging a strong spiritual connection with God. "I was very much aware of

Hashem. And I always wanted to continue my studies. The teacher prepared me in order to be certified as a Hebrew and Judaic Studies teacher. I learned Torah and Hebrew. I wanted to know everything to do with the language and the history." Carla continued her religious learning, even while later attending nursing school in her teen years, before the Nazis invaded Holland on May 10, 1940.

1930

Scholars estimate that approximately 106,723 Ashkenazic and 5,194 Sephardic Jews, in 1930, lived in the Netherlands, with roughly 90,000 Jews in Amsterdam.[9] *The Jewish community was fragmented, without leadership. "By the 1930s, most Jews felt themselves to be very well integrated into Dutch society," writes Holocaust authors Deborah Dwork and Robert-Jan van Pelt in their work,* The Netherlands. *"The mild genre of anti-Semitism that prevailed in the Netherlands must be understood within the unique context of Dutch society, itself a collection of fragmented groups, none of which can claim a majority. These minority groups or 'zuils' were seen as 'columns' on which the state rested. Each zuil had its own political party, newspaper, trade union, schools, university, sports societies, and broadcasting system. However, where there was a Catholic, three Protestant, and two secular zuilen, no Jewish zuil existed. This was due to the size and fragmentation of the Jewish community. What unified these different groups was the House of Orange, the country's* monarchy, which represented the glorious history of the Netherlands. All groups, including the Jews, shared the history of the Dutch Republic. Therefore, Jews perceived themselves to be, and were recognized by their Christian countrymen, as 'Nederlanders.'"[10]

During the early 1930s

Dutch Jews were confronted with the need to care for the tens of thousands of Jewish refugees who had fled to the country due to pogroms and anti-Semitism in Germany and other countries in Europe. In Holland, these refugee needs were addressed through the Committee for Special Jewish Affairs.[11] While a more virulent strain of anti-Semitism articulated in the Netherlands throughout the mid- to late 1930s, the Dutch were rather reserved with regard to Nazism, and many rejected it completely. As elsewhere in Europe, however, Nazism was perceived as a preferable alternative to Communism, which was greatly feared.[12]

1931

Anton A. Mussert founded the National Socialistiche Beweging der Nederlanden (NSB), Dutch Nazi Party on December 14, 1931.[13]

1933

January: Adolf Hitler was sworn in as chancellor of the German Republic.
March: First concentration camp in Germany, Dachau, was established near Munich.
April: Establishment of the Gestapo under Nazi control in Germany.[14]

1934

The Nationale Juegdstorm (NJ), National Youth Troops— the Dutch equivalent of the Hitlerjugend, Hitler Youth was established.[15]

1935

January 7: Italian fascist dictator Benito Mussolini and French foreign minister Pierre Laval signed an agreement between Italy and France that paved the way for cooperation in the event of action by Germany.

September 15: Nuremberg Laws established: Reich Law of Citizenship and Law for the Protection of German Blood and Honor decreed at Nazi Party rally in Nuremberg. Laws provided that only persons of "pure German blood" could be citizens, and prohibited marriage and extramarital relations between Jews and Germans.

1937

January 30: Hitler associated Jews with Bolshevism.
March 15: Joint Boycott Council organized Mass anti-Nazi rally in New York.
July 16: Buchenwald concentration camp was opened.
August: Approximately three hundred and fifty attacks on Jews in Poland occurred.[16]

* *

Carla was not an ideal student at the gymnasium. although her parents were unaware of her lack of academic drive. The school suggested that Carla repeat the third grade of gymnasium, but she had lost all interest in school. She was focusing on a career. "I was eighteen. I said to my parents that I would like to be a nurse. For an Orthodox Jewish girl, there were not many options. It was also rather peculiar to have one child, and she goes off at eighteen to pursue nursing."

But the combination of nursing and Orthodoxy was not a conflict for Carla. She did not live the life of a cloistered observant Jew. She lived, played, attended school, and studied with Jews and non-Jews while, in tandem, maintaining and nurturing her Orthodox upbringing. "My religion was always with me."

Once Carla announced that she wanted to study nursing, her father explored the opportunities available that would accommodate Carla's religious observance and offer an excellent nursing experience.

In Amsterdam, where approximately two-thirds of the 140,000 Dutch Jews lived, there were three Jewish hospitals. Carla's father went to the largest, the Central Israel Ziekenhuis or CIZ, and asked how to go about becoming a nurse there. The CIZ directed Carla to apply in Het Apeldoornsche Bosch, a Jewish psychiatric institution. "Since my parents had nobody who was mentally ill, they agreed that I should apply there. It is important to know that a lot of Jews had mental problems because of intermarrying [within families] in Holland, especially in Amsterdam."

In 1935, at the age of eighteen, Carla began her nursing studies, undertaking a three-year training commitment at Het Apeldoornsche Bosch. The Jewish psychiatric hospital was located on beautiful grounds approximately within one hour's walking distance from the city of Apeldoorn. For a time, Carla and Tetta lost touch.

**

As a nurse in training, the culture at the hospital was one of learning and camaraderie. The Jewish hospital had a kosher kitchen. However, Carla remembers that the food was atrocious. "It was horrible. And not so good for the patients either!" Consequently, during the week, she and her friends barely ate, maintaining a diet of mostly peanuts. Carla's parents had no idea of her poor eating arrangements. Each week, for Shabbat, they sent her a traditional meal that she graciously shared with her fellow nursing students. "My father wanted me to have the same food that he and my mother ate on *Shabbos.*" Sometimes, Carla was required to work on Saturday, but she never complained.

A few months into her studies, Carla was assigned nursing responsibilities in the coveted small private "pavilion." This building was smaller than the other hospital housing on the Het Apeldoornsche Bosch campus. It housed the wealthy patients who could afford to pay outright for their hospitalization. A desired position for the nursing students, Carla had a room to herself. She has fond memories of her studies there. In particular, she found a mentor in the pavilion nursing adjunct, a nurse named—Siebert, a German. Carla describes her as "being stricter and more dedicated." Nurse Siebert was a Seventh-day Adventist who was not well-liked among the staff. But Siebert liked Carla, and took her under her wing. Additionally, Carla liked the director of the facility, who was also German.

As a nursing student, on her days off, Carla would go into Apeldoorn and visit her friend Erna Leefsma. The girls knew each other before Carla moved to Apeldoorn through Agudas Yisrael (Society of Israel), a Jewish teen/youth organization that held *Shabbatonim,* organized Orthodox Jewish youth group gathering that had programs, including lectures, prayers, and Jewish studies. During these get-togethers, Carla also became very close with Ben-Zion Hirsch. From Zwolle, Ben-Zion was Carla's third cousin, a descendant of the great rabbi, Meier Joune Hirsch. Eventually Erna and Carla decided to form their own weekly study group. Erna's family lived with her mother, Ro (Rosa) Elzas, and three other siblings. Erna's uncle, who also lived in the town, was very knowledgeable in Talmud, Hebrew, and Torah and agreed to teach the weekly meetings. The girls, including Carla's friends Eva Sanders and Junt Manus, cousins Walter and Remie Elzas, and a few others attended. The topic was *Shulchan Aruch:* the explanation and study of the observance of *halacha*, Jewish law. Through this study group, Carla had her first encounter with a young cantor, Andre Andriesse.

Andre Andriesse used to travel by train weekly, from Aalten to Apeldoorn to visit his cousins, the Elzases. There, he would stay with his "Tanta Ro." During these visits, he also attended his cousin Erna's study group.

Carla noticed Andre "right away." Erna told Carla that Andre was interested in her as well. They met officially for their first date on October 10, 1937. Their dating was a proper courtship of mostly talking and taking walks together, "because that's the way it was done in those years." From that first date in October, Carla met Andre every week at the Apeldoorn train station.

Andre Andriesse

*S*he taps her Droste's chocolate box. In it are marked envelopes filled with pictures. The dates on the back of the photograph are old, dating from the 1920s. Also inside are handwritten index cards from interviews with the Shoah Foundation, the United States Holocaust Memorial Museum, and Yale University. The sepia-tone photographs are arranged in neat piles. No yellowing edges or frayed paper. In the Droste's box are also photos of those who shared the experience of the Holocaust. Unfortunately, many in the box never lived to even have one single memory of this horrific attempt of complete Jewish annihilation.

One photo is of Andre. It is inserted into his identification card that was issued to him by the Nazis, one week before he was arrested. The card looks brand-new.

"I'm sorry, I don't have many pictures. I lost so many during the war," Carla explains with a small lilt. Thoroughly, she scans each photo, and remembers better and more quickly than my laptop can retrieve a single file. We go over each picture. Each has its own history that is rich and resonant with stories and musings. Some escaped, hid, emigrated, survived. Others were rounded up, arrested, transported, shot, gassed, murdered, or committed suicide as a result

of the pain. These photos do not reflect that intangible reality. As for Carla, it is not luck, but because of Hashem that she is here today to tell me her experience. She knows this is important. I know we are on borrowed time.
The Droste's box goes into my bag.

Andre, from all the photographs, was a very handsome, dark young man. He was born in the small town Cuyk a/d Maas, in Branbant in the Netherlands. According to Carla, many Jewish cattle handlers lived in this region. He came from a *frum* (religious) family. His maternal family was the Elzas family of Borculo who, in the 1800s, ran a successful business of making parchment from cow leather. Due to family dynamics, Andre's grandfather, Walter Elzas, left the business. It continued to thrive under the management of his brother, who passed it on to his sons, Nathan and Moses.

Carla explains that it was common practice in the late 1800s for frum Dutch men to go to Germany to secure frum wives. Both Nathan and Moses followed this cultural tradition. Andre's mother, Eufemia Elzas, had two brothers and a sister named Ro.

Andre's parents, Eufemia and Joshua Andriesse, met in Cuyk a/d Maas, courted, and were married. They had three children: Andre, Lies, and William, known as Willy. Andre was five years old when his father Joshua passed away. Eufemia was then left with the three children.

Emotionally, the responsibility was too much for her to manage. Today, Carla explains, she probably would not be seen as stable or fit enough to raise children. What were the options for a widow with three children and little financial help? Sending children to an orphanage was a common practice when a family was struggling. Incapable of raising the three children on her own, Eufemia decided to send Andre to a Jewish orphanage in Utrecht. The director and Andre formed a close bond. His experience at the orphanage was positive, with hard work, learning, singing, and given the circumstances, having fun.

After thirteen years of living in the Utrecht orphanage, Andre went into military service. As a draftee, he became an officer. Upon completion, he returned to Cuyk a/d Maas, most likely to be with his mother and siblings and support the family.

Andre's sister Lies, younger than Carla, became a nurse in Het Apeldoornsche Bosch, the same Dutch Jewish psychiatric institution where Carla studied. Willy, Carla surmises, was mentally retarded; therefore, as an adult, he continued to live at home.

Carla recalls that Andre had a good voice. He pursued and eventually secured a job as a cantor. "I suppose it was his training in the orphanage and on his own that led him to this profession," Carla explains. In 1936, he took on the position of cantor in the small town of Aalten, located in the province of Gelderland. The town had a small Jewish community in which most of the Jews worked in the cattle business.

Every week, Andre Andriesse visited his Aunt Ro and cousins in Apeldoorn where he met Carla.

The attraction was immediate and mutual. Carla called her parents and told them that she wanted to become engaged to Andre. They rejected the idea. The Nathanses spoke with knowledge and authority.

Carla's parents were well-respected members of the Assen community. Their devout Jewish lifestyle included the mitzvoth of hospitality, *haschnosas orchim,* practicing kindness, *chesed.* This act of hospitable kindness was once extended to a young cantor who was traveling through their town. While the Nathanses were chatting with the young cantor, Andre Andriesse, their conversation subject settled on the town of Apeldoorn. The Nathanses and Andre realized that his cousin, Erna Leefsma, and Carla were friends. This coincidental visit was Andre's first, albeit unofficial, meeting with his future in-laws.

Andre explained his family history, sharing the fact that his mother was not well. This information, combined with his status as a cantor lead the Nathans to object to the courtship. If Carla would marry Andre, she would have the added burden of caretaker. For these reasons, the engagement was not allowed.

Although Carla's parents refused to condone the engagement, Carla was steadfast. "I didn't care. I told my parents, 'too bad.' Imagine, I was an only child!"

The term "engagement" did not imply the final step preceding marriage. For Carla's generation, the term was to imply dating. In the case of Carla and Andre, her parents did not allow her to even say that they were "engaged." Neither was it acceptable to simply start dating someone. "That was not our way of living. You didn't just date without a proper announcement of engagement." It was word-of-mouth knowledge that enabled courtships to move along in a socially appropriate formal Dutch manner. As a result, Carla and Andre's relationship had no official endorsement. However, in their eyes, they were committed.

During the winter of 1937, Carla's mother became ill a few weeks before Carla was to take her nursing exam. On December 31, Carla, in Apeldoorn, received a phone call that her mother was seriously ill with pneumonia. Carla immediately went back to Assen; and as a result, she was unable to take her nursing exam.

In Assen, as a daughter and nurse, she tended to her mother's needs until she died. On January 7, 1938, Johanna Hartog Nathans's last words to Carla were a request: "Promise me that you won't marry Andre." "I said that I could not do that. Imagine. I was twenty."

At her mother's funeral, Carla and her father discovered that Johanna was financially supporting Gentiles in need. "We had no idea. We didn't know about it, but that was the case. This is to show that she did not do things only for herself. She just didn't know how to express herself on a personal level." During shivah, Carla's father still tried to convince her to give up Andre. Carla did not listen. Emotionally exhausted, she returned to Apeldoorn, feeling unprepared to tackle the makeup exam. "I said to a doctor that I couldn't pass it. But he encouraged me to focus hard and attempt it." Carla eventually took the exam and became a certified *verpleegster*. Her badge was a small black cross. Over that hurdle, Carla applied and was accepted into the nursing program at the Jewish Portuguese Hospital.

1938

Dutch borders are effectively closed to Jewish refugees. New arrivals were returned to Germany. Exception: After Kristallnacht, regulations were relaxed for a short time in which seven thousand refugees were allowed into Holland. The Dutch government required the Dutch Jewish community to care for the refugees. Thus, Westerbork, the internment camp for German Jewish refugees, was built by the Dutch government. The Dutch Jewish community paid for its construction and operating costs. The leadership of the loosely termed "Dutch Jewish community" allowed this to happen. No one dared to criticize the Dutch government's policy. During their centuries of citizenship, the Dutch Jews had learned to expect protection from "above," and they were not suspicious of national authority or their own leaders. The system had worked well for nearly three hundred year, and the trust it had engendered blinded the Jews and prevented them from realizing that the very system would be a tool for their destruction. In short, the Jews were like other Dutchmen and reacted to the Germans like other Dutchmen: they were, for the most part, cooperative, *administratively efficient, and loyal to the authority; and they assumed that their leaders had the best intentions.*[17]

March: The Anschluss: Germany incorporated Austria into the Reich.

May: First group of Jews began forced labor in Mauthausen.

August: Jewish men in Germany were required to add "Israel" to their name; Jewish women were required to add "Sarah."

September: Munich Agreement: England and France allowed the annexation of parts of Czechoslovakia by Germany.

October: Fifteen thousand Polish-born Jews were expelled from Germany to Poland; most were interned in Zbaszyn, Poland.

November 9-10: Kristallnacht: in retaliation for the assassination of Ernst von Rath, a German secretary in Paris who was shot by Herschel Grynszpan, whose parents were expelled from Germany in October to Zbaszyn, Poland, Joseph Goebbels instigated pogroms in Germany and Austria. In one night, 267 synagogues were destroyed, 7,500 stores were looted, and thirty thousand Jews were sent to concentration camps. Ninety-one Jews were killed.[18]

* *

Ultimately, Carla's father gave the engagement and wedding his blessing, with one stipulation: a job proposition.

Near the German border sat Enschede, a large factory town with a Jewish community of two thousand, large in comparison to Carla's hometown of Assen. Joseph Nathans proposed that if Andre secured the position of assistant cantor at the city's synagogue, the marriage would have his approval. Andre and Carla agreed to these terms. Andre applied, interviewed and was hired. Carla declined her nursing position at the prestigious JPH (Jewish Portuguese Hospital) in Amsterdam. Carla and Andre married on August 26, 1938 at her parents' friends home, the Mendelsons. "It was a natural choice. My father had since remarried, Bep—, and moved from Assen to Amsterdam. I actually did not have an *elderhouse* that I could marry out of and these people were like parents to me." In attendance were the TECALEI group, represented by Carla's friend Leida, Andre's cousin, Erma Leefsma, and childhood friend Emil Mendelson. In addition, her beloved cousin Ben-Zion and a handful of extended family also came. No music was played during the reception because Carla was still in the *aveilous/ ovel*, year of mourning for her mother.

With Andre in the position of cantor, the young couple settled into their home the same day of their wedding. Attached to the splendidly designed Enschede synagogue, it was to be the center of their social, professional and religious life. The home was elegantly furnished by Carla's father with antiques he had kept in storage from the house in Assen.

> The kitchen in that place was huge. It was designed with the function of being used also for the synagogue's caterer, if necessary. Our plates and service were all from Assen. The bedroom furniture was all new. There were two large bedrooms. The third floor had two rooms, one occupied by the girl who worked for me. The dining room was done in my taste. The salon's décor was furnished with fine antiques chosen by my father.

The home's furnishings did not reflect Carla's personality, but having no money of their own, the couple was, of course, grateful.

"When we were finally installed, my father said that our house was big enough more for people and he wanted to move in with us. I did not like the idea right away because I knew that my father would be the boss and I wanted my husband to be the boss," Carla explains. "My father was quite upset, but I told him no and he had to take it. See, I am not a nice person," Carla says this repeatedly about her opinions and actions.

The Andriesses settled in. Andre's role as assistant cantor, teacher, and administrator set the couple socially apart from the rest of the Jewish families in Enschede. However, another family preceded Carla and Andre's move to Enschede by six months, the de Groot family, Philip and Juut and their two children, a boy and a girl. Philip de Groot was the *shochet* (ritual butcher/slaughterer) and a teacher in the Hebrew school. The two families became friends. In Holland, the clergy was paid by the state, and consequently, independent of the congregation. "Socially, you were a little on your own if you were the cantor of a congregation. That's how it was in Holland. So that's why we became close with the shochet family."

※ ※

November 9, 1938, would later become etched in world history as Kristallnacht. Carla and Andre heard firsthand of this dreadfully horrible night from a German couple who fled from Germany to Holland the next day, November 10.

> Two people came into the shul and told Andre and me what happened the night before. They said that they saved themselves by lying on the roof of their house. The interior of their home was destroyed. We found a place for them to stay.

Once this couple had a place to live, whether it was in an abandoned home or a rental, they had to obtain identification papers, food stamps, and other necessities. Andre was an integral part of this safety net of people who aided those who fled.

Carla explains that lots of German Jews escaped to Holland via the rivers that intertwined the borders of the two countries. As the Jews desperately entered Enschede, Andre obligingly placed these stateless persons in different homes. Carla explains that Andre and his connections could place up to ten people in one place. These individuals were not necessarily "hiding," although they were not supposed to be in Holland either.

1939

January:
>Illegal immigration to Palestine from Germany began. Twenty-seven thousand German Jews immigrated by the end of 1940.
>
>In a Reichstag speech, Hitler threatened to exterminate the Jewish race in Europe if world war should once again break out.

April:
>Italy invaded Albania. Conscription began in Britain. Legislation enacted allowing for the eviction of Jews by German landlords.

May:
>Ravensbrück concentration camp for women established. British government issued the MacDonald White Paper that restricted Jewish immigration to Palestine.

September:
>Invasion of Poland by Germany. Two million Jews came under Nazi rule: one hundred thousand Jews served in the Polish army fighting the Germans.

Britain and France declared war on Germany.
The United States declared its neutrality in the war.
Gestapo decreed that Polish Jews in Germany were to be deported to Dachau.
Jews ordered off the streets in Germany by eight o'clock each evening.
Red Army occupied Vilna, Lithuania, home of fifty-five thousand Jews.

October:
Poland surrendered.
Nazis established the Generalgouvernement, the civil administration for those parts of Poland not incorporated in the Reich. Hans Frank was appointed governor-general, and decreed that all Jews ages fourteen to sixty must serve two years of forced labor.

November:
Nazi ordered all Gypsies in Germany deported to concentration camps.
Hans Frank, governor-general of Poland, ordered all Jews in the Generalgouvernement to wear yellow stars and mark Jewish businesses with yellow stars.
Heinrich Himmler ordered that Jews refusing deportation be put to death.

December:
Nazis began using gas vans to murder mental patients.
Nazis cut food rations for Jews in Germany.[19]

**

In 1939, German intent was horribly clear. Carla's community heard of the Nazi's action on the radio, from the newspapers, and firsthand accounts from German Jews who made their way to Enschede, located precariously close to the German border. Psychologist Eva Fogelman explains in her essay "The Rescuer Self" that Dutch society was "aware that Jews were losing their civil liberties, most interpreted this change as temporary, not as fatal, and not necessarily as warranting intervention."[20] Little by little, the Nazis began to infringe on Carla's life.

On July 20, 1939, one year after they were married, Carla and Andre had their first child, Channa. In Enschede, where their life and family were supposed to take root, establish, and grow, Carla's world began to fall violently apart.

In August or September 1939, as new parents and one year into their marriage, Andre was recalled into the army. Carla, with the baby and a girl in her employ to do household chores, stayed behind in Enschede. Andre corresponded weekly with Carla. After a few weeks, his correspondence ceased. Carla knew that something was wrong. Andre was stationed in Alkmaar, not far from Amsterdam. She called her father, who was living in Amsterdam, and said she was coming to meet him so they could both head to the army base and find out what was happening to her husband. Together, Carla and her father took the one-hour train ride north. Her instincts were right. "I had a sixth sense." Andre was in the infirmary and very ill with pleurisy and a high fever. Carla spoke to his superiors, explaining that the congregation needed him because it was nearing the high holidays. The military did not discharge him based on Carla's word. But in the interim, the Enschede Synagogue had petitioned that he be discharged based on religious obligations. After a few days of bureaucratic paperwork, the couple boarded a train for a rough two-and-a-half-hour ride home.

When they returned, Carla immediately called a doctor. "Penicillin had just come out about a month after my mother's death." After a few weeks, Carla had nursed him back to health. Due to his obligation to the synagogue, Andre never reported back to his military service.

1940

January:

Ovens and crematoriums were installed at Buchenwald concentration camp.

Jews in the "Generalgouvernement" were prohibited from changing their residence or leaving their homes between nine at night and five in the morning.

March:

Nazis ordered that the letter J be stamped on food ration cards held by Jews in Germany.

Transports arrived at Nazi concentration camp Sachsenhausen, north of Berlin, from Nazi concentration camps Dachau and Flossenbürg in Germany.

Polish youth beat up Jews and defaced Jewish property. Nazis observed and took pictures.

April:

Denmark and Norway invaded by Germany.

Generalgouvernement Nazi leader Hans Frank ordered that Krakow, Poland, be made "Judenrein," free of Jews, by November 1940.

Heinrich Himmler ordered the establishment of a large new concentration camp near the Polish town of Ocswiêcim, known by its German name, Auschwitz.

May:
Rudolph Höss was appointed commandant of Auschwitz.
May 10: Germany invaded Belgium, Luxembourg, and the Netherlands.
Neville Chamberlain resigned as prime minister of Great Britain and was replaced by Winston Churchill.
Nazis began deporting Gypsies to ghettos in Poland.
The German occupation authorities banned Dutch Jews from civil service, and required all Jews to register the assets of their business enterprises.
May 13: Queen Wilhelmina and her government fled to Britain.
May 15: The Netherlands surrendered.
May 17: Germany invaded France.
Heinrich Himmler recommended to Hitler that Polish Jewry be deported to Africa.
Evacuation of 338,226 Allied troops from Dunkirk began.

June:
Norway surrendered.
At the Topf works in Erfurt, Germany, a model of an oven for incinerating human corpses was made.
Italy entered the war on the side of the Germans.
Germany occupied Paris.
Soviet Union annexed the Baltic States.
In France, Vichy Government was established: Marshal Philippe Petain formed a collaborationist French government in Vichy.
France signed armistice agreement with Italy.
Soviet Union annexed parts of Romania.[21]

Autumn 1940:
Germans demanded no more Jews be admitted to the civil service.

November 1940:
All Jews were dismissed from civil service in Holland. Students from two of Holland's nine universities went on strike in reaction. Dutch Nazis, representing 1.5 percent of the population, were told to foment street riots against the Jews in all big cities. During these riots, a Dutch Nazi was killed. In retaliation, the Germans brutally and viciously rounded up over four hundred Jewish men and boys in full view of Jews and non-Jews alike. They were deported to Mauthausen in Austria. Most died.[22]

**

Throughout 1940, Carla and Andre's life continued under a tight cloak of nerves and fear. The Netherlands sits vulnerably on Germany's western border. Although separated by a land border, the Netherlands' vulnerability lay in its labyrinth of rivers, canals, and channels. The country's defense of these waterways was the equivalent of using lace to stop torrential hurricane winds from bursting every window in your home. Before the official Nazi invasion of the Netherlands on May 10, 1940, many German Jews escaped to the Netherlands. The Dutch army did their best to defend its bridges from the Nazi invasion with the Waterlinie, a project that deliberately destroyed strategically important bridges. However, the Dutch neglected to think "up." The Luftwaffe bombed the country with countless air raids—the sounds shake Carla's memory with acute clarity. "I can still see it happening," she says, pointing in the air to the warplanes she remembers seeing and feeling fly overhead. "I remember my girl was vacuuming in the living room, and we heard the airplanes coming over. We could hear planes dropping bombs. It was scary. Much later and slowly, the Germans began forcibly removing Jewish people out of their houses."

On May 15, 1940, the Netherlands surrendered.

**

A hard knock at the door woke up the Andriesse family during a cold winter February night in 1941. "I was terrified. I begged Andre not to go downstairs to open the door. But he said that he had to open the door. I remained upstairs with the baby. I heard a lot of noise."

It was the Gestapo.

"I took the baby out of the crib and went up to the third floor, where the girl's room was. Across the hall, doors led to the roof." Wearing only her nightgown, Carla, with the baby in her arms, escaped to the roof. "We had a flat roof. It was covered with ice and snow two feet high. But I went out with the girl who was staying with us. I thought to myself, 'Maybe I can jump down.' But there was no way. There were searchlights and Gestapo everywhere. We just stood in the cold. And stayed for several hours."

After a freezing agonizing wait, Carla says that she heard a faint, soft voice. It was Andre. Carla climbed back inside.

> So I went downstairs. I met Andre in the dark, halfway up the staircase. We said, "Let's get out of here. They could come back any second." We were scared to death. It was after twelve when the Gestapo came in. Or maybe it was two thirty or three o'clock in the morning. I have no idea anymore. Andre explained that they came with bayonets. They pushed Andre, as far as I know—I was on the roof. I only know what he said to me. Because it was a synagogue, they wanted the Sefer Torahs. That was the first thing a Jew thinks of protecting. Andre thought to lead them through the hallway that connected our house to the synagogue office. Andre knew that in the office, there was a safe that contained an old Sefer Torah that was no longer used. Whatever happened, I don't know. He said, "They got spooked. All of a sudden, they

ran." Whether they were *shickered* or just chickened out, I don't know. One or two of them went upstairs and opened my armoire and stole all of my jewelry. Some of it was antique, from my family. We only discovered this the following day, after we returned to the house. Behind the kitchen there was a storage area. The baby carriage was there, and that's what they used to carry out the loot.

That night, still fearing that the Nazi soldiers would return again, Carla, Andre, and Channa retreated to the synagogue's main sanctuary, taking the same hallway where Andre had led the drunken soldiers. In the back of the dark, freezing cold hall, they hunkered down under the grand main sanctuary's gallery. "We crouched in the miserable freezing cold, underneath the balcony of the women, and sat there until the sun rose the following morning. It was very cold." At five thirty in the morning, the Andriesses, still dressed in their nightclothes, went to their neighbors, the head cantor and his housekeeper. "We went there to defrost and tell them what happened. They were startled because we woke them and it was so early in the morning. I am sure they were still sleeping."

Carla did not feel safe sleeping in her home. "Under no circumstances was I going to sleep in that bed." The Andriesses found a temporary place to stay with their cousins, the Weil family. This lasted for three days. "We were too many people and we were not welcomed there. We looked around for a different place to stay. We found a place across the street with the de Leeuw family. They offered the attic. And that's what we took. We were saved for the moment." This arrangement lasted for seven months.

1941

The process of isolating Dutch Jews from the general population was intensified through 1941. The year was devoted to the systematic undermining of the situation of the Jews in the Netherlands. The final objective was evident from the outset. In the Netherlands, no provisional experiments were implemented. It was unlikely that the new rulers of Holland, all SS officers, were unaware of the end aim of the preparatory measures they were implementing.[23]

January:
> German authorities required all Dutch Jews to register as Jews. A total of 159,806 persons registered, including 19,561 persons born of mixed marriages, termed "Mischlinge." The total also included approximately twenty-five thousand Jewish refugees from the German Reich.[24]

February:
> *The Jewish Council of the Netherlands,* or De Joodsche Raad was ordered established by Hans Rauter, SS head in Holland. It was composed of the Jewish bourgeoisie.[25] This method of establishing Jewish Councils was a calculated step in the Nazis' process of murdering the European Jewish population.

February 22:
> Nazis began arresting Jewish males in Amsterdam as a result of clashes between Dutch Nazi supporters and Holland's Jews. Jewish men were arrested and deported to Mauthausen concentration camp near Salzburg, Austria, where they were killed.[26]

February 25:
> These mass arrests lead Dutch non-Jews to respond in the form of a general strike in Amsterdam. "De Joodsche Raad," fearing Nazi retaliations, demanded the strike to stop. Thus, the first (and only) massive non-Jewish opposition in Europe in support of Jews ended with the support of Jewish leaders.[27]

May:
> The concentration of Jewish property began according to a plan drawn up on May 19, 1941, at a meeting of all the heads of the German administration in Holland. The Nazis' plan concentrated Jewish capital and used it to finance the Final Solution. Dr. Hans Fischbock, the expert who had already organized the looting of Jewish property in Austria, carried out the detailed planning of the operation.[28]

August:
> Kosher slaughter of animals was outlawed in the Netherlands.

September:
> Jews were ordered to transfer all sums of one thousand gulden or more to the Lippmann bank, formerly under Jewish ownership, now controlled by the Nazis.[29]

October:
> All Jewish businesses were ordered to register with the new government. All Jewish financial holdings were registered.[30]

Not the Only One

In Nazi-occupied Holland, *razzias* (mass round ups of Jews) were carried out in order to capture and annihilate the Dutch-Jewish population. These were the same *aktions* (roundups or mass arrests) that the Nazis organized throughout the war, a calculated methodical step in their very organized plan of mass deportation to the concentration camps. In Holland, men, women, and children would be arrested en masse, corralled into a large area (perhaps a stadium, town square, synagogue, or park), and then shipped to a transit camp, such as Kamp Westerbork.

In 1939, just south of Assen, Kamp Westerbork was built by the Dutch government and funded by the Jewish community. Ironically, it was to be a place of refuge for the German Jews fleeing from their homes. Instead, the Nazis used the camp as a convenient collecting point, a transit camp, for shipping Dutch Jews to Auschwitz, Mauthausen, Sobibór, Theresienstadt and Bergen-Belsen and ultimately their deaths. Some of the more provincial Jews were sent to Kamp Vuhgt, in the south of Holland, before being shipped and murdered.

The Nazi's concentration camp system that had the ultimate goal of murdering its prisoners consisted of using transit camps to corral the Jewish victims and then dispatching them by train to slave/forced labor work camps, ghetto or extermination camps.

On September 13, 1941, a razzia was unleashed in late afternoon in Enschede. It missed Andre because he wasn't at home; he was in shul, praying. There were windows in the attic where we stayed. We could look out and see our house from there. That's important because this is connected to when they picked Andre up. On September 14, we were sleeping in the attic by the neighbors. It was very early in the morning, we heard and we saw them across the street at our front door: a Gestapo and the Dutch NSB (*Nationaal-Socialistische Beweging*, Dutch Nazi Party), the Fascist, he was in normal clothes. I heard the bell ring across the street. Then they left the front door. I said to my husband, "They are coming to get you." We knew about what was happening in Germany. "And that's it," I told him. "Don't go out." The Gestapo knew that there would be at least ten men at the shul. This day, September 14, happened to be *Selichot*, the seven to ten days before Rosh Hashanah. Special prayers are recited during morning services. Services start earlier to allow time for these additional prayers. So *Shacharit* (morning services which normally starts at seven) was going to start at six thirty in the morning, meaning that Andre had to get up earlier. So I told him, "Don't go to shul. They are coming for you." He said, "No, I have to go. I belong to the congregation. They count on me. I have to go." And he did. And of course, the Nazis came back to the shul during services. I have no idea, really, how many they

> picked up there. I never actually knew how they picked up the other people. I don't know how they picked up my father. I don't know how the razzia was really conducted. I can't tell you that. All I know is that I was worried about Andre. I was dressed, I came down into the street, and I saw them (Andre and the men from services) coming out of the shul and going down the street. I walked a little bit behind them with the child in my arms. It was no use to go anywhere. I was standing there, watching them going, going, going. There was a woman standing next to me, she was from Germany. She said to me, "What can you do? You are not the only one. I got furious at her." They didn't get the *shochet*, Philip de Groot. He sneaked out the backdoor. I don't know if they were brought to the lyceum or the police station, but I think it was the lyceum.

Carla and Andre never made eye contact.

The Nazis picked up Andre and marched him to the police station. "There was nothing I could do. I was just standing there with the child in my arms, looking at him." All Carla could do was turn around and go back to her house with Channa.

Philip de Groot escaped the razzia. He and his wife, Juut, came to Carla's home to console her for the next few days. Carla's cousin, Ben-Zion Hirsch, also came to comfort her. "He was like a brother to me. He would bring coupons that I could use to buy more than was allowed at the time." Carla felt no need to continue sleeping in the attic across the street. If the Nazis were coming back for her, she no longer cared. She was numb.

> After Andre was taken, a rabbi made a visit to Enschede, and of course, he could only partake by

me. We had a conversation over lunch with Juut, in the living room. I still see him sitting there. I didn't open up so much. He said, yes, there are some people that cannot show their emotions. I realized that is the type of person I am. I could not stand in front of him and cry. I may eat it all up inside. I am strong. But that doesn't mean someone else can't be a different way.

The Nazis used Jews who held leadership positions in their communities as pawns in organizing and carrying out their mission of Jewish degradation and annihilation. The guise was that of a committee. Mr. Siedfrid Menko, who was a successful textiles businessman and president of the Enschede synagogue's congregation, was enlisted by the Nazis to "serve" on the Jewish Council. His home was transformed into the Gestapo headquarters. He was assigned the responsibility of contacting family members of those who had been picked up and informing them of their loved one's death. According to Carla, the Nazis instructed him to bring the families of those who were "rounded up" to the Gestapo headquarters so they could publicly hear the names of the dead. On October 17, 1941, Mr. Menko notified Carla by phone that Andre was killed at Mauthausen She was to report to Gestapo headquarters to hear his name read in order to be publicly humiliated. "It was very cruel. I told my friends that I would not go. I would not give them the satisfaction. I didn't care. I said to him that I was not going to go, and I didn't. After I was told about Andre on October 17, we (the Jewish community) were informed by the president that no one had to hear the names anymore. This was because of Hashem. Hashem helped me not to face the dilemma that I had to go."

A few weeks after the razzia, Juut and Carla discovered they were both pregnant.

**

A couple of weeks passed in a fragmented and disjointed fashion. Pragmatically, the community had to find another assistant cantor for the congregation. Mr. —— de Vries was appointed. Carla was informed via telephone that the de Vries family wanted to move in as soon as possible; Carla and Channa were being asked to leave their home. Carla protested to Mr. Menko, the president of the congregation. He firmly told her that she had to vacate the house.

> I thought, how does he dare throw out a pregnant wife of twenty-four and a child out of their house into a street? This man was a multimillionaire, making his fortunes from the lucrative textile industry in Enschede. But I didn't care. I gave it to him point blank. "How dare you put someone in this situation on the street?"

Both parties, the president and the pregnant widow, went back and forth. Finally, Menko asked the de Vrieses if they could all live together for a while until Carla could make other arrangements. "So we made a compromise; I could live upstairs until the second child was born. I am still surprised. How did I dare talk so boldly to someone with such stature and respect in the community? Okay, it was not my house; it is part of the synagogue. But you still feel it is your home." During the winter months of 1942, living with the de Vrieses was a necessary, and obviously, uncomfortable arrangement.

Carla's grief gripped her with a melancholic despair. She operated robotically, day to day. Her mind was a blank slate. "I never thought about being pregnant. I never thought of the child. Never. Not until I was seven months pregnant." She and Channa shared two rooms and financially scraped by with Andre's small pension.

In April 1942, Carla found a place to live on her own in the outskirts of the city. It was far from her small circle of friends including the de Groots. However, Carla had to move on. She secured a rental of two rooms and a kitchen from a Jewish family named Samuels. The de Groots lived in town, close to the shul and the Ziekenzorg Hospital. As Carla's pregnancy progressed, Juut suggested that she come and stay with her back in the city.

> This way, it would be a shorter walk to the hospital once my labor began. I eventually moved with the Juuts' neighbors, the Palache family. They had a small house, but they made space for me. It became *Pesach* (Passover). Juut gave birth to Menachem in March 1942. In the meantime, there was still a curfew. At the end of Pesach, I felt that I was getting ready to give birth. Once my labor began, a girl who lived with the de Groots walked me to the hospital at night after the curfew.

As Carla approached the end of her pregnancy, she arranged for her father and his wife, Bep, to care for Channa. While in their care, they took the baby to the wedding of Carla's cousin Ben-Zion and Renee Nathans. "He would have loved to marry me. I heard this from a friend. But he married my cousin, Renee Nathans." The photographs from the wedding are the last pictures that Carla has of her father.

1942

Germans announced that every Jew found in hiding would be sent to Mauthausen. In fact, not a single one of those who were detected were sent there; most Dutch Jews were deported either to the concentration and extermination complex of Auschwitz-Birkenau or to the extermination camp of Sobibór in eastern Poland.

January:
> *Forced-labor camps were established in Holland. Jews were forced to relocate to a ghetto in Amsterdam.*

March:
> *"Aryanization" began. All Jewish businesses were taken over by Gentiles during the next two years. All Jewish property was turned over to the Nazis including stores, jewelry (except wedding rings) and bank accounts. Travel was forbidden without official authorization.*[31]

> *"De Joodsche Raad" The Jewish Council understood that the German Jews were being deported to "labor camps" in Eastern Europe. But the council took no action. They*

believed the German Jews would be the only Jews sent out of the country. They were deeply shocked when, after the introduction of the yellow star early in spring of 1942 and not a single German Jew had yet been deported, they were told that Dutch Jews would be deported East as well. All of them? No, the Germans said, Jews whom the council deemed important to carry out its many social activities would be allowed to remain in the Netherlands, at least for the time being. The council fell into a well-designed trap.[32]

April:
All Jews ordered to wear a yellow badge: a star, with the word "Jood" in the center of the star.[33]

May
Dutch Jews' right to a legal defense was officially revoked.

June 30:
A curfew was declared from eight o'clock in the evening to six in the morning. Shopping hours were restricted. These limitations were joined by prohibitions against working in any economic field and any branch of medicine or related professions.[34]

July:
Mass deportations began.

July 15:
First trains left for Auschwitz. On July 18, 1942, Heinrich Himmler was present at a selection of Dutch Jews when this first train reached its destination.[35]

From July 1942, Germans assumed that they would deport all so-called full Dutch Jews within fourteen months. Basically, they did. There was no resistance on the part of the Jewish Council.[36]

December:
Letters and postcards to families from Jews deported to Auschwitz-Birkenau, and not selected for the gas chambers, arrived in Amsterdam. Forced to write the deceptive correspondence, the letters informed families that they had arrived safely and that living and working conditions were tolerable. Many of these letters were not passed on, but several batches did arrive in Amsterdam from the first deportees that left Westerbork.

End of 1942:
When train traffic was halted from Holland to Auschwitz, 38,571 Jews were dispatched. [37]

**

Carla takes a sip of her tea. She says it helps with her digestion. The tea is not strong. She says that someone in her family told her it is not healthy to drink so much tea. But, she tells me, it's so weak. She's not going to listen to them anyways. Carla does not complain about her ailments. Once, I walked into her kitchenette and saw the entire table covered with little white-lidded bottles of medicine. I was shocked.

At eighty-seven, Carla has the wisdom of acceptance. If she's in pain, why complain too much; what's it going to accomplish anyways? I've never seen her upset. Because she has such a firm love for Hashem, everything has a reason. There are no dark corners in Carla's philosophy. Regardless of the miracles or tragedies in her life, all are created within the parameters of Hashem's plan. Embracing this divine arrangement makes her world easier to accept. Her willingness to welcome whatever curveballs are thrown her way surreptitiously seeps into my attitude. I'm not so quick to melt down at the crisis de jour. My reserve of patience has grown.

Behind a Funeral

When I was pregnant, I felt it would be a boy, but it was a girl. I wanted the baby named Joshua, after my husband's father. My father suggested that she should have a special name. So she was named Jedidjah: *Jedid* means "beloved," and *Ya* means "the Name" for Hashem. It was really a boy's name, but . . . oh well.

Carla's and Andre's daughter, Jedidjah was born April 12, 1942, at Enschede's Ziekenzorg Hospital. Nazi records released ten years after the war indicate that Andre had already been dead for six months.

"The doctor was great, very compassionate. He stayed with me after the birth because he knew that my husband wasn't there anymore. He was an older Jewish man." Carla's father came to see her and the baby right away. Although the Nazis had issued strict curfews, her father was still able to make the train trip from Amsterdam to Enschede.

Carla stayed in the hospital for two weeks. While she convalesced in bed, she was issued the yellow star to wear. "You couldn't get out of the hospital without it. I sewed it on my jacket. I remember it was a brown jacket with wide lapels and a matching brown skirt. I guess you got three or four stars. You had to wear it so you could see it. If you wanted to wear something different, you had to change it and sew it on something else. You didn't think much about it because everyone had to do it, too. And no one would talk about the star."

With her star neatly sewn on her jacket, Carla clearly remembers leaving the hospital, pushing Jedidjah in a baby carriage. She and the baby, along with her father and Bep, walked back to the small place where Carla now lived.

In the small apartment she rented from the Samuels, she merely existed with Channa and Jedidjah. In a period of intense bleakness, she does recall lighter moments. "Once, I came back from the pantry with our meal and I found Channa had given the baby of about three months some bread! She must have heard her crying and thought she was hungry. I was so alarmed to see the infant in the crib with crumbs all over her mouth. I'll never forget it."

A couple of months passed. In perhaps June or July 1942, Carla heard that the Nazis were going to round up women. How did she hear about these impending razzias? "From friends or from other people in other cities." Carla's father had already been arrested and was interned at Kamp Westerbork. Carla does not know the details about how he was taken to Westerbork. More than likely, Joseph Nathans was rounded up in a razzia with other Jews in Amsterdam.

During the summer of 1942, Carla began to consider hiding. "You can't imagine what people tell you about the camps is true, but it is. And because of that, I decided that I was going to hide." Her father only wrote once from the Kamp Westerbork, telling her that he did not believe what was happening in Germany. In his sole letter, he gave Carla his bunk number so that she could find him. Her father was also absolutely against the idea of hiding, insisting she not do it. "He also felt that nothing could happen to him—only to other people. He was living in denial. I think it is a good way of living, in a way, right? I don't know that he was that frum that he thought God would help him. I don't know. I can't look into someone else's soul."

Meanwhile, Carla's girlfriend, Juut de Groot, heard that there was a minister in Enschede by the name of Overduin. Juut heard that this gentleman was dedicated to helping Jews. She also heard that the Nazis had killed his brother. Carla went with Juut to see him at his house in August 1942.

> Hiding was not popular at that time. Right away, I picked up that Dominee [minister] Overduin was helpful to other Jews. It was kind of known in Enschede that he could be trusted. Of course, Juut and I were scared to death. After Andre was taken, I was scared all the time. So it was only because I was so scared that I thought about hiding. The minister said that he'd try to help us out. He had a group of people that would help him but nobody knew anybody else. He really stuck his neck out. He knew that if he got picked up he'd be killed too. You have to be very faithful and believe that God will help you.

The Nazis occupation of the Netherlands was marked by terror. The five-year occupation never let the Dutch resistance get firmly organized. Open dissent could easily lead to immediate execution, particularly later in the war, when Germany knew that the Allies were closing in on them. However, some brave Dutch did hide Jews.

Most people hid Jews out of deep moral convictions. Others did it for money if the Jews could pay. Different people became involved in the resistance for very different reasons. Carla observed that sometimes good, lucrative business relationships could lead to Gentiles hiding their Jewish clients. In other circumstances, friendly neighbors would take on this dangerous risk. But Carla's world was more insular, being the wife of the Orthodox cantor. Although she had non-Jewish friends, she was not close enough, even to ask her childhood friend, Tetta, for such a grand sacrifice.

Unfortunately many Dutch citizens collaborated with the Nazis, betraying Dutch Jews, leading to their deportation. Why? In some cases, the Dutch were financially rewarded. In others, they did it for free. No one wanted to be overtly associated with the Jews. It would be suicide. Anti-Semitic hated of Jews was encouraged.

"The Nazis would kill the Jews and Dutch people who hid them. The Jews were killed on the spot if they were found, or they were sent to concentration camps," Carla flatly states. Somehow Carla and Juut were informed that someone found a place for them to hide.

"Channa was the biggest security threat because she could say, 'My mom is in here or there!'" Therefore the minister had to find a place for Channa first because of her ability, literally, to talk. Sometime in the beginning of October 1942, Minister Overduin and his underground organization found a place for Channa. His instructions were clear-cut: Carla was told to bring Channa to the Enschede train station and a man, a complete stranger, would pick her up.

> I meticulously packed everything that I could, thinking of everything that the people might need for her. For instance, I packed thread and other items like this, because things were getting quite scarce. Imagine what it is like packing for a child to go to someone you don't even know? I took Channa by her hand and pushed Jedidjah in the carriage, and we went to the station. I put the suitcase for Channa at the foot of the carriage, and Channa walked next to me. She didn't know what was going on. I didn't explain things. I thought I was walking behind her funeral. I didn't know if I'd ever see her again.

Carla gave her to a man whom she had never seen before and never saw again. The stranger, taking Channa's hand in his own, and her neatly packed suitcase in the other, boarded a train for an unknown destination and fate.

Carla's life was disappearing. Channa Andriesse was taken to a kind family in Veenendaal, in central Holland. "They were a Christian family, and the father was a principal of a high school. Before I went into hiding, I received pictures of Channa from the family, via the organization. I found out later that Channa persistently asked for me. They told her that I was ill and couldn't take care of her."

With Channa hopefully in a safe place, Carla now needed to disappear into the Netherlands *with* Jedidjah, a difficult task.

In November 1942, the organization found a couple who indeed would hide the baby; but Carla was the obstacle. Carla explained that Resistance contacts—she assumes they were women—explained to the couple that there was a baby *and* her mother who needed hiding. The organization's contact asked the couple if they would take both people—mother and child. They reluctantly agreed, telling the women that if they had to "think it over" then the answer to hiding both would be no.

Grudgingly, Jan and Pauline Mulder agreed, at an enormous risk, to hide a Jewish woman and her six-month-old child. Sometime in the beginning of winter 1942, Carla and six-month-old Jedidjah left Enschede for the tiny village of Marle, Overysel.

With No Thought of the Future

They traveled, Carla thinks, by car. "I went to Marle, a *gehucht*, just a place with several farms spread around. They had a farmhouse. It was next to the elementary school where Jan was the principal. He was also an *imker*, a beekeeper. His wife, Pauline, had been a schoolteacher. It was November 1942."

What is the scene of a hiding life? Only with hindsight can the imagination conjure up the first time Carla walked up the steep stairs to her attic accommodations. Now part of an underworld over the first floor of the Mulders' farmhouse, Carla was part of a hidden anti-community. Cut off from her eldest daughter, removed from her friends, alive when her husband and father were dead, her ascent with each step was driving her further underground, severed from her world. "I was to stay with Jedidjah in an attic room on the second floor that contained a crib, bed, chair, and small dresser. The room had one window and no heat." Carla spent most of her time sitting in that room, alone.

> There was no communication or contact with anyone. No signal. No knocking. And there was no way that I could go downstairs by myself. No way. Pauline would

> not let me come downstairs if anyone else was in the house, which was rare, or it felt unsafe. I was sitting all by myself, going crazy. I wasn't thinking of being freed again. There was no information from outside. I was *davening* a little bit. I didn't think about the war . . . how it would go. I only knew that my husband was dead.

Carla could never ask to use the bathroom; she was dependent on Pauline for relieving herself. Some days Carla was not allowed to use the bathroom at all. After sometime, she asked for a pot in which to eliminate. She could urinate in that but was unable to have a bowel movement. "I always had to wait until it was safe to go downstairs to use the bathroom."

This was an enormous problem throughout Carla's hiding, leading to serious illness during the war. Even today, she is racked with major intestinal and digestive health problems that can be directly related to her hiding.

> Sometimes I took the pot and would go out on the roof at night. It was very cold. I wore clothes layered over each other. Before hiding, I had made a jacket that was pretty warm. You have to understand that you had to take everything that you could possibly need with you wherever you went. I cannot remember a shower or anything. I can't remember when I could wash my entire body. Pauline must have brought me a little hot water. I do not recall all that. That's terrible, but I don't. Understand, in Holland, showers were not done. You took a bath in a bathtub.

On an occasion where Pauline felt it was safe, Carla would go downstairs to use the bathroom, eat, or to help out in the kitchen. Carla remembers making butter with a churn and talking with Pauline. Carla recalls that the conversations were rather sophisticated, not what she would expect from a typical provincial farmwife. For Carla, these recollections were a measured bit of brightness in an increasingly ominous environment.

The Mulders rarely received visitors. Sometimes other farmers from Marle came with food. No one appeared to know that Carla and Jedidjah were there. Pauline slowly became paranoid that Jedidjah, barely a half of a year old, could talk and tell visitors that Carla was hiding upstairs. "She wasn't yet forming words." Carla knew that she was incapable of telling anyone anything, let alone revealing her existence.

Carla became convinced that Pauline was unstable and wanted Jedidjah as her own child. "I do know that Jedidjah liked Jan. He was a nice man. I don't know how far Jedidjah's memories go back. Pauline was definitely in charge of that household. She insisted that Jan use a cloth napkin when they ate. Can you imagine, during such times?"

Pauline was no cook. Eating arrangements and mealtimes were abnormal; Carla and Jedidjah were fed when it felt safe. Jedidjah was given warmed leftovers from the previous day, mostly porridge. "Whatever vitamins were in the food before were gone by then." Carla, being religious, never ate meat even if it was available.

Pauline concocted a miserable porridge of unground rye with milk. "This type of rye," Carla remembers, "you couldn't cook it long enough to get it to soften." The results of this unhealthy diet, coupled with the tense anxiety, led Carla to her first bout of gastro-intestinal illness. "In the spring of 1943, I got sick on account of my poor diet. My large intestine got infected, and they had to call the doctor." Thus began Carla's suffering with her intestines and entire digestive system.

> The doctor was a "good" one. He had to have some connection to the underground, or he couldn't have come into the house. He told them that I had to stop

eating that stuff. He was additionally stunned by Jedidjah's deteriorating condition. When the doctor came to visit to diagnose me, he reprimanded Pauline and Jan about their obvious neglect of Jedidjah. Her health was also deteriorating due to the poor diet and lack of sunshine and fresh air. They never let Jedidjah go outside. Ever. He said to them, "What's the matter with you? This child has rickets!" He told them to get her outside in the sun and give her oranges and vitamin C.

By the time the doctor was called to the Mulders' home, Carla's role as a mother had been completely usurped by Pauline. What happened? Although Pauline was a teacher and therefore educated, Carla surmised that Pauline did not possess or use a lot of common sense. Carla recalls that her actions bordered on the bizarre. Her nurturing skills were peculiar. Her reality was skewed. Why she was hiding both of them, Carla was unsure. Jan and Pauline did not want money from Carla. "They would certainly be killed for taking money from me." Crystal clear to Carla was the fact that Pauline wanted a baby.

Pauline's encroachment was gradual. When Carla and Jedidjah arrived in Marle, Jedidjah slept in the crib in Carla's room for approximately six weeks. The first couple of weeks, Pauline brought the baby's food upstairs to Carla. "By that time," Carla recalls, "Jedidjah was eating, no longer just on a bottle. In the beginning, when I had Jedidjah I fed her myself in the room. I remember that she would begin to cry when she heard me scraping the bottom of the bowl. But I had nothing else to feed her."

Sometimes, Carla would spend a short time downstairs to feed the baby, help out, or eat with the family. After about three months, Carla was told to stay upstairs and Pauline took over all the baby's feedings. "Pauline began to take the baby out of the hiding place more and more frequently. I hardly saw her. What could I do? Not only that, she also took Jedidjah *and the crib* out of my quarters and moved her to the Mulder part of the house, also upstairs."

After a certain period of time, Carla rarely saw her child. Sometimes she could hear Jedidjah cooing when Pauline brought her to bed because the staircase was next to Carla's room. "They called her 'Didi.'" Eventually by January 1943, Carla was not allowed to see Jedidjah at all. "I couldn't complain and say the baby was not in the room anymore. I was twenty-five. Pauline was in her thirties. That's it. Okay." Carla slices her hand through the air.

Pauline took the baby into her world and pushed Carla further away. How did Pauline explain the appearance of a baby to others? "Of course, then you could adopt," Carla explains. "She could have said this, or that the child was simply from relatives." Distant relatives, for sure. Jedidjah had dark, dark hair like her father Andre. She looked nothing like Jan or Pauline. Carla remembers Pauline cutting her hair extremely short so that her appearance would not give her away.

"They scalped her all the time."

This was Carla's life for approximately two years.

Go Back to Bed

I was sitting in this room all by myself, day in and day out. I didn't have much to do. Of course, I had no radio. Most people didn't because it was against the law. I think that Jan may have had one near the end of the war. I had taken yarn along with me. And later, Pauline gave me more. I knitted and knitted. Then I knitted and ripped it out and did it again. Before I went into hiding, I also bought about twelve little small cans of sweetened condensed milk. If I were really hungry, I would carefully take a spoonful. Eventually, the milk supply was depleted. They had a library at the school. She also gave me books. They were very, very frum Christians.

Carla recalls that people from the organization/resistance came to the Mulder's home about five or six times. "You could usually tell if someone came because it was an unusual feeling in the house," recalls Carla. They brought food ration stamps for flour, sugar, and butter. The Mulders, living among the farmers, were not heavily dependent on these ration stamps. "They didn't need it so much, but okay, they could use it." Carla remembers only being allowed to see and talk the contacts on two or three occasions. "Pauline didn't even think that my speaking with these people was important to me." Carla carries deep resentment for these missed opportunities to connect with the underground organization. But she tempers her frustration. "Remember, it was also a big chance that the Mulders took. They could be killed also. You have to see this from both sides. But that being completely understood, Pauline still operated in her own reality."

The psychology of those who hid Jews follows no simple pattern. Carla's experience, like each Jew who hid, is unique. Both Jan and Pauline have passed away; I cannot ask them directly for their own personal reasoning. Research shows that these people did share the trait of independent personalities. Minister Overduin and the contacts in his network each had his or her own reasons for defying the Nazis. Carla knew that the Nazis killed the minister's brother. This could explain his personal motivation.

In addition, "Some Christian rescuers saw in their Jewish charges as only hunted and persecuted human beings. These rescuers recalled that it was their suffering more than anything else that prompted them to help," explains Holocaust survivor and sociologist Nechama Tec in her essay "Reflections on Rescuers." "Coming to the aid of Jews who 'belonged to a despised minority' was a way to stand up for what was morally right."[38]

The Mulders' path to becoming a rescuer was common: Most people who were involved in hiding the Jews "did not initiate rescues on their own. A friend, an acquaintance, or a friend of a friend came and asked for help,"[39] *writes Eva Fogelman. Without this "domino effect" of hopeful aid, would Carla be here today? Probably not.*

Carla was instinctively smart to get out of Enschede when she heard about the razzia for women. Being the assistant cantor's wife, her name would have most certainly been on the roundup's list. *These mass arrests were carried out quickly and methodically, "before there was time to think, much less act," explains Tec. The Mulders made an on-the-spot decision to take both mother and child. This quick decision-making process was also typical behavior during the Holocaust. As Carla recalls, her underground contact told her before she went into hiding that if the Mulders had time to think it over, the answer to taking both Carla and the baby would have been no. However the Mulders' commitment to hiding Jews was shared with approximately twenty-five thousand Dutch families, according to the premiere Dutch holocaust scholar Louis de Jong.*

> How many non-Jewish families had the courage to open their homes, and often their hearts too, to their persecuted co-citizens? We do not know exactly. In some places, only one Jew was given shelter; in others, ten or more. In some places, Jews stayed only for a brief period; in others, for nearly three full years, each of which seemed endless. One Jewish child was given shelter in twenty-four different hiding places. My estimate is that the number of homes where Jews were kept hidden may well have been twenty-five thousand, and my further estimate is that there were at least two to three thousand resistance workers whose main or exclusive activity consisted of finding hiding places, papers, food coupons, and money for Jews in hiding, and of solving their endless and often nerve-racking practical and personal problems. Some of these Righteous Gentiles, as they are called by the State of Israel, have been honored by the Yad Vashem Institute in Jerusalem. Most of them did not receive, nor did they claim, any recognition. Their conviction was that they had merely done their duty as human beings, and in the contacts I have had with members of this group, it has struck me that many of them felt they had not done enough.[40]

The psychological motivation of those who hid Jews runs the gamut of reasons. Some did it to make money, which was risky because that arrangement could also lead to death. But with the stakes so high and money and food being so scarce, if a Jew had the means to pay, the quid pro quo was worth the risk. According to Nechama Tec, "I refer to them [those who took money] as paid helpers, not rescuers."[41]

Surprisingly, some rescuers were blatant anti-Semites with a guilty conscience, and others were Jews. However that does not accurately explain Carla's experience. Jan and Pauline Mulder did not want any money from her.

"Some of them [the rescuers] mistreated their charges by starving them, demanding more money, and sometimes even threatening them with denunciation and death," writes Tec. Carla reiterated that there was not always compatibility with the hider and the hidden. "I learned after the war that Andre's Tanta Ro Elzas from Apeldoorn was almost killed by those who hid her. They probably wanted more money... She wasn't the easiest woman to get along with. I didn't even know she was hiding until after the war." However complicated the sociological interaction between the rescuer and the Jew, the dangers and risks of accepting the responsibility of hiding a Jew were ominous. If caught, both rescuer and Jew were doomed to torture and death. Countless Dutch Jews never made it out of their hiding place or home alive.

Was Pauline's desire to be a mother the driving force? Perhaps. But that cannot be the whole story. "The ability to see beyond Nazi propaganda, to strip away the gauze of Nazi euphemisms, and to recognize that innocents were being murdered lies at the heart of what distinguishes most rescuers from the bystanders," explains Fogelman.

Placed deeply in these individuals' psyches must have been some modicum of hope. Resistance requires hope. "As a rule," Tec writes, "hope tends to fade with grave danger. Danger without hope saps the will to struggle."

End result, hiding was inconceivably dangerous.

"What else can you do?" Carla would often comment. Widowed, separated from her first child, Channa, cloistered in an attic, and stealthily robbed of mothering her other child, Jedidjah, Carla spent her days trying to keep occupied: reading and rereading books, knitting, and re-knitting with yarn. Although cut off from the news of the war, Carla was soon to find that the poison of Nazism was welcomed right in the heart of the Mulders' home.

"Pauline trusted her family," Carla explains. "Her uncles and aunts and everybody. She told them about me. They were Christian Scientists. They were marvelous people. They would come and talk with me. They had their religion, and I had mine, and we respected each other. They were very intelligent. They did a lot of good for me. It was about twice they came to visit. How they are truly related to Pauline, I don't know."

Then came another visitor: Pauline's mother.

She came for one or two weeks in the spring of 1943. Pauline told Carla that she was coming. In previous conversations, Pauline informed Carla that her mother was a Nazi.

And now the Nazi was coming to visit.

"That was a big problem for many obvious reasons, one of which, I couldn't come downstairs at all."

> There is this artificial dual existence. So I am not there. They have a baby, and the mother is not to know I am there. The mother has the room opposite the stairs downstairs. I was not allowed downstairs, but sometimes I just have to go to the bathroom. It is five in the morning, and I have to go. In order to go, I have to pass by the mother's room. I have to open the door of the staircase, which is exactly opposite the mother's bedroom. I

make it to the bathroom and am sitting on the toilet. The mother comes, and she wants to go also. Well, so I am sitting there. I said to myself, "Hashem, what am I going to do?" Hashem gives me in my mind that if she would see me, she could have a heart attack on the spot because she does not know that I am in the house. After a while, in my mind comes the fact that I can make believe that I am her daughter. I made my voice a little lower. I said, "Mom, I am not ready yet. Why don't you go back to your room, and I will come tell you when I am ready." This is what the man or the woman upstairs tells me. It's a chance, right? A very big one. But it is what Hashem has in mind for me apparently. So I say this. To my *mazel* [luck], she goes back to her room. I hear her go back. I don't know how far back. I didn't know if she would really go to her room. She could just be waiting right outside the bathroom door. After all, it's dark. She's an older lady, in her eighties. But it's cold. Maybe she will go back to her room for that reason. I come out and try to run to the staircase door. I had made some type of knitted socks or slippers, which kept my footsteps quiet so no one could hear anything. So now I come back to her bedroom door, knock on the door, and say I am ready. I have *mazel* that there is a door in front of the staircase. You cannot imagine the tension that was there. All these things are coming back to my physical health problems today. Everything that I have is projected by Hashem. I feel that strong that everything that happened to me—good and bad—is always part of Hashem's plan. I have this through my whole life.

Whether it was Pauline's mother, soldiers, or neighbors, Carla never knew who could come and disclose her hiding. For both Carla and the Mulders, their life was a shared terrifying existence. The Mulders sensed this Nazi danger on several occasions. "Though I don't think the farmers in Marle even knew that we were there, you couldn't trust anyone. Your best friends could turn you in." In order to physically hide Carla, Jan Mulder, who was very handy, had made a secret hiding space for Carla.

> This was done very early because it was necessary. He made a false interior wall with a small entrance that allowed access to a space between the roof's interior rafters and the interior of the house. I would creep into this dark space located between the wall and the studs. There, I would wait. At times, when the Gestapo would travel the roads, I would hide for hours in the dark with not much air. It was very cold. Pauline once hid Jedidjah in a small cabinet like that for a long time, as well. Jedidjah told me this later.

The stress of the situation, compounded by Pauline's commandeering of Carla's mothering of Jedidjah, brought Carla to a precarious tipping point.

"In the beginning of 1943, someone came from the organization and I was allowed to visit with her. I told her that I couldn't take it. I didn't care anymore. I would go to the camps. I could be killed. I couldn't take it anymore. This was a dangerous thing to let someone come out of hiding because this person, if caught, would be made to tell who everyone is in the organization."

The woman suggested that maybe an additional woman could be brought in to lighten and diffuse Carla's frustration. The Mulders agreed to accept another Jew, thereby adding more immense risk to their situation. The contact explained that this other person and Carla would have to sleep in the same bed. A few months later, the organization brought an older woman, someone who could be the age of Carla's mother. She was more of a rough woman, not a person with whom Carla could have a conversation.

She was always full of so-called jokes. There was no finesse in the woman. She was not a bad woman. I came from Gymnasium. I learned all kinds of languages. She only knew Dutch. I am just trying to convey what type of relationship you can have with this person. She was Mrs. Wijnberg.

"So I had to sleep with her in one bed. She was fifty-four. And I had to accept it. I couldn't do anything about it. It was not really what I had hoped for. She went downstairs more than I did. She got along well with Pauline. She could kid around with her."

1943

By July:
> Otto Bene, the Nazi Foreign Ministry representative, reported proudly that the one hundred thousandth Jew had been removed from the midst of Dutch society.[42]

September:
> In total, fifteen hundred letters and postcards from camps were passed on to the Jewish Council. The council found it disquieting that there was not a word in these letters that referred to the wives, the children, and the older people who had accompanied these male camp letter writers when they left Westerbork. A few of the letters did have clear and courageous warnings, but these were disregarded.[43]

September 28:
> Just before Rosh Hashanah, the last great razzia was conducted in Amsterdam. Among the two thousand Jews taken from the Jewish Theater to Westerbork were the heads of the Jewish Council.

March:
> Most diamond workers were deported, apart from a small group who were taken to Bergen-Belsen in order to practice their craft.

1944

Summer 1944:
> The last of the Jewish Council officials were deported.[44]

September 17:
> Strike of the Dutch railway men began, the day the Allied Airborne Army land near the big rivers (the Lower Rhine), which cut off a small part of the country and lasted for eight months.[45]

* *

The Offer

Around June 1943, Pauline said that she and Jan were going to a wedding and wanted to take "Didi" along. "'We found someone to take care of you,' Pauline explained to me, 'He is a sheriff in Marle.' I don't remember their names. That is very bad because these people are so very important, but I am sorry." Carla had no exact memory of how she made her way with Mrs. Wijnberg to the sheriff's house, but surmises that they must have walked at night.

> First of all, the sheriff lived in a two-story house. When you came upstairs there was a small landing. When we arrived, they had a table and chairs set up, with all kinds of goodies for us. Next to that was the bedroom. They didn't want the goodies in the bedroom. I don't know exactly what time of day we came. It was just terrific, like a hotel, so to say. That's why we felt it was paradise. The Mulders were only gone a very short time, so we didn't go downstairs or anything. The bathroom must have been upstairs. I think we arrived in the late afternoon and the Mulders left the next day. I told them that I came from the eastern part of

Holland. The couple had either one or two children. The lady of the house was in her mid-twenties, a bit *zaftig,* and had a younger sister living with her at the time. I did not even know their names because of the danger. This couple knew that Pauline Mulder was strange. The Mulders were involved with the organization, so I knew their names but this is different. I want to emphasize that when in hiding, you couldn't know too much about the people who were involved because that was another risk, another danger.

Pauline came back in less than a week, and Carla and Mrs. Wijnberg returned to the Mulders'. "So the only thing is that we know that other normal people are alive! When we left, the lady of the house said to me that anytime that I would get into trouble I could come back to them. That message sustained me through the *whole war.*"

Carla and I sit down in late July 2004. As always, Carla has a glass of water chilled for me, a pillow for my back in my chair, hard candies in her tiny petite filigree silver basket, and her notes. Fresh cut blooms from her bougainvillea and rose bushes spray out from a little vase and complete our table. She, petite and graceful, is always so neat and well dressed. Her pretty glass beads always coordinate so well with her clothes. She wears a shaytl that is light brown with hints of gray. I always admire her fashion. Remember, she is approaching ninety years old. Her aches and pains abound. She has survived so much. And yet she puts together a great ensemble, wears her make up tastefully, and smells so good. Conversely, I barely get there on time. No make up, frizzy hair and overheating in the Florida summer humidity. Wearing pants, which is a bit disrespectful but a least a step up from my shorts. I'm lucky to remember my watch. There is a syncopation to our routine by now. I look forward to the work. Today we tackle tough stuff: leaving the Mulders. We've discussed her experience before. But now, knowing Carla for over a year, it is time to fill in the blanks. Dig out the emotion.

It is not easy.

In early 1944, a woman came to the Mulders from the underground organization to make a check on Carla's situation and give ration coupons to the Mulders. Carla was allowed to speak with her and asked about her close friends Juut and Philip de Groot. The woman told her that Juut and Philip were no longer hiding, but had obtained fake identification and were posing as a minister and wife. The contact told Carla that Juut, a brunette, was now blond and did this by using peroxide on her hair. "That was new. In those years there were no cosmetics or other products for coloring one's hair." Carla, desperate to leave the Mulders, decided that she would try to change her identity as well. "Juut and I were always told we looked a lot alike, so I figured that I could take the risk as well. I was so fed up hiding that I decided to try what Juut and Philip did. I was going to change my appearance in order to get out of hiding."

The Mulders were not happy that Carla was going to take this risk because it added yet another level of danger to being discovered. "I didn't care. I wanted out. You better believe it. I knew it was risky. There comes a time that you don't care anymore and that is a dangerous time. Your judgment is not clear. You see no future. You become so depressed and distressed that nothing matters anymore. But that's how I was. I didn't care."

In preparation for her dangerous departure, Carla needed to create a new 'un-Jewish' appearance, obtain false documents and secure a safe destination. Carla asked Jan to buy the peroxide. "I do not know if I had money with me but I must have had. I do not know these details anymore. You were so totally erased from your environment that you don't even care."

Carla used the peroxide every morning, "I had a little bottle and I put the peroxide here and there on my head, starting in the front of my head."

After several months the color started to become lighter. "Pauline and Jan said nothing about my hair color. They probably thought I was crazy."

Finally, a contact from the organization came and told Carla she would be getting a new identification card. One obstacle remained. She needed to be photographed for the bogus paperwork.

In September 1944, Jan found a minister in Nijverdal, not too far from Marle. His home would be a drop-off and pick-up point while Carla was in Nijverdal obtaining a necessary photograph. Was the minister also involved in the organization? Carla does not know. "Everything was so secret. The whole idea in hiding was that you shouldn't know what was going on around you, in the world, or anywhere. So I didn't know the name of the minister in Nijverdal. How I got there, I don't know. There were no cars. I didn't go on a bicycle. It is totally vague to me."

> Before going to have my picture taken, I had to go the beauty salon. It was all arranged with the organization, not me. I was just like an animal, but I didn't mind. At least all of a sudden I was among other people. The contact said that I would have a permanent before the picture. You have to understand, you didn't know or do anything. I was like a lump. So dumb. I see myself sitting there. I see the girl putting the conditioner on my hair and putting on rollers that were attached to a machine. That is how it was done in those years. The beautician does this, and after five or seven minutes, she checks to see how it is going to see if it is taking. She takes one rod out and attempts to unroll it. As she pulls the rod away from my head, the hair stays on the rod!

There was no strength left in Carla's hair. Her poor diet combined with the peroxide left nothing but a weak excuse for hair for the beautician. Carla recalls that the beautician felt terrible. She began to frantically take out the rollers, going as quickly as she could. "I was laughing. Not crying. What ever will be, will be. The whole situation was too overwhelming in a way. I was worried only about survival." Carla does not know if the people in the beauty salon were aware that she was a Jew. "The entire beauty shop took a moral risk by having me in there."

Carla ended up with a very short, cropped haircut. She doesn't remember who or where she took the photo for her forged identification. After the hair debacle and photo session, Carla headed back to Marle. It was several months before she finally received her new identification. At that time, the contact informed her that she would be going to Utrecht. How, exactly when, to whom? Of course, Carla had no idea. "I remember the last meal I had with the Mulders. Jan read a special part of the Bible. It was Psalm 121. I was impressed. It was very appropriate. He was a very nice man."

I raise my eyes upon the mountains; whence will come my help? My help comes from the Lord, Maker of Heaven and earth. He will not allow your foot to falter; your Guardian will not slumber. Behold, he neither slumbers nor sleeps-the Guardian of Israel. The Lord is your Guardian; the Lord is your Shade at your right hand. By day the sun will not harm you, nor the moon by night. The Lord will protect you from every evil; He will guard your soul. The Lord will guard your departure and your arrival, from this time and forever.

"I didn't know what would happen next."

I constantly press Carla for her day-to-day thoughts while hiding, for any description or anecdote that could funnel her fearful existence into my tools of understanding. Besides listening, this is my best way to get my bearings in her world. She seems to have a pattern that we both acknowledge: Her articulate and clear recollections are insightful. Her lack of memory on other occasions also speaks loudly. If Carla did not have control of the situation, she has no memory of how it evolved. "That's because I had no input," she explains. "It was important that everyone involved in the organization knows as little as possible. The more knowledge you had, the more dangerous you became."

The lack of control in her life and the drone of constant fear make me nauseous. It gives me headaches. The juxtaposition of our interviews sandwiched between my mundane trips to the grocery store or rounds of errands makes for a queasy mix.

But I am not complaining.

"To live in fear, twenty-four hours a day, to fear you will get caught. You weren't in Auschwitz, okay. But which is worse?" The question Carla asks is rhetorical, but I am sure it haunts survivors who successfully hid during these hideous times.

It is very difficult for Carla to pinpoint how long she was in hiding with the Mulders. She estimates the dates to range from approximately November 2, 1942, to October 1944.

By deciding to leave the Mulders, she also left her daughter. How did she justify her decision to leave? For practically two years, she was not allowed to see her child. In addition to losing her husband, her home, and identity, she was no longer allowed the privilege of being a mother.

She saw no future.

However, her decision to hide had, so far, kept her and a daughter—maybe both—alive. The physical tolls and mental costs were incomprehensibly mounting: illness, depression and despair, lack of any control, and, now, complete separation from Jedidjah. "You could say that it was selfish of me [leaving], but I couldn't think that way. I didn't know if the war would *ever* be over." Carla does not recall if she was even allowed to see Jedidjah before she left.

> All of this took time. I became very restless. I had to wait for the organization. It was very frustrating because I never knew when or if I would hear from them again. How everything happened, I don't know these things. That is, in a way, the sad part. There is a lapse in my memory. How this whole thing is arranged or developed, I don't know. I did not initiate it. I was ruled and regulated by others. But somehow I made it to the train station and went from Marle to Utrecht. There was no train station in Marle so someone had to bring me to Nijverdal, but I have no memory of it. I must have had money, but I don't remember. I don't remember if anyone gave me any. If you ask me why and how, I don't know how these things happened. I know that I had to have some money because I took the train. No one gave me any money, but I had to have had it somehow. I have to emphasize that the danger of being picked up was everywhere. I was in fear constantly.

In mid-October 1944, Carla arrived by train in Utrecht with her forged documents and no child. Carla's identification papers read Henriette Andriesen. "It was both a Jewish and non-Jewish name," she explains. But again she had no input in this decision. She went "to a lady who had a three-story boarding house." Carla must have had an address and an explanation of how to get to this place, but she has no memory of this either. The neighborhood was familiar. Utrecht was home to her uncle Abraham "Braham" Nathans. Carla was to be a maid.

> I was in hiding for two and a half years without much nourishment. I looked as though I came out of the concentration camp. I couldn't function properly, attending to three floors with three flights of stairs. After a week or ten days, I got very sick, but I never went to a doctor, of course. Next to the room where I was lying down, there was a woman. She wore a nurse uniform, but I don't know if she was a nurse or not. Maybe she was Jewish herself. She may have been trying to act like a nun. She had pity on me and said, "You cannot stay here because the lady of the house has a lot of Jewish borders, they pretended not to be Jewish in their everyday lives. And it's just too dangerous."

This "nurse" found a less-risky place in Maarssen, a suburb of Utrecht, with a doctor and his wife. There, Carla could be their maid. "Why did she trust me and why did I trust her? This is Hashem who does this for me." The arrangement did not last long. At first, the doctor and his wife could afford to share their food, but after a couple of weeks, Carla had to go to the soup kitchen. "You have to realize that we lived in Holland, and it is a small country. The Germans took everything they could get. Some farmers near the eastern part of Holland, near the German border, grew potatoes and grain. People would travel by bicycle to the east of Holland to get a sack of potatoes or whatever they could barter or pay for."

In the soup kitchen, the only thing to eat was cooked sugar beets. "From that you could get very sick."

Carla's stomach troubles became worse while in Maarssen. Andre's murder, the separation from Channa and Jedidjah, and poor health were dead weights on her clandestine existence. Carla was desperate, flat-out depressed, constantly living in fear, and getting sicker every day.

> From the couple in Maarssen, I wanted to get back to this sheriff's family. This was January 1945. I heard that there was a truck going to the place where I wanted to go in the east. I wanted to go back to these people. I explained to the doctor and his wife that I was going to go back east. It was very difficult to go because the Germans controlled all the bridges, and trucks were constantly searched for illegal activities. But I had no other choice. I went in the back of a truck overnight on February 1, 1945, with about fourteen or fifteen other people. A young couple and I began to talk. They didn't know I was Jewish. The truck was headed to Zwolle, the capital of Overysel, the same province of Enschede. This is where the young couple lived. They said I could stay with them in Zwolle until the curfew was over, from the night until the next morning. While on the road to Zwolle, the Gestapo soldiers stopped us and came in the truck. They asked for passports and ID. They wanted to know why we were in the truck. We told them that we needed food and we heard that there was food on the other side of the country or something like that.

Thanks to Carla's formal education and her mother's background, she knew perfect German. "It was like a second language to me. I also knew French, Greek, and Latin. I learned all these languages at the gymnasium. So I answered in German. It was as easy as Dutch to me. The soldiers did not ask anything more of me because they assumed I was a German woman. Again, Hashem's hand helps me."

> I believe we arrived in Zwolle during the curfew, in the early dark morning hours. I went to the couple's house, had tea, and I left at seven o'clock that morning. I didn't want to stay too long because I didn't know where I would end up. My mind is set to go to back to Marle. But I know that I couldn't make it in one day. It was February 2, 1945. The snow was piled high, and underneath it was a solid coating of hard ice. I had nowhere to go except back to Marle, to the sheriff's house. So I began to walk all day.

Carla figured if she made it that day to the village of Nijverdal, at the home of a minister, where she had spent a few hours before being taken to have her hair done and pictures taken for identification, well, then she would be halfway to Marle. "I thought it was a safe place." She calculated the walk from Zwolle to Marle to be about forty miles. She would need to rest. She would, perhaps, stay safely until the next morning and then continue to Marle.

> I must have had a suitcase or something. It was very dangerous because nobody was walking on the roads. Only trucks with Germans were on the roads. The roads were primitive, no asphalt. They were made with gravel and sand, and topped with dirty ice and snow. They didn't have the transportation and major roads. Maybe you'd see a hay wagon or something, but that's it. I must have had to walk twenty to thirty miles in cold and snow, from seven in the morning to three in the afternoon, from Zwolle to Nijverdal. I arrived at the minister's home and knocked on the front door. I asked if I could stay for a little while. The minister said no. They didn't want me. I asked again.

But they didn't want to hear from that. I don't even know if he offered a cup of tea. So I had to go on.

Carla arrived in Marle the same day she left Zwolle, at seven o'clock in the evening, February 2, 1945. Clutching her suitcase, her small frame layered with meager clothing to protect her from the brutal winter, Carla walked forty-three miles through snow that blanketed an ice-encased Dutch landscape. No food. No water. For twenty-four consecutive hours, Carla aimed for survival, based solely on a kind offer. "This is the thing that is very sharp in my mind."

As she made her way back to Marle, Carla passed the Mulders' house, where her baby, Jedidjah, was, more than likely, fast asleep.

When she approached the front door of the sheriff's house, she remembers feeling faint. After Carla knocked on the door, an unfamiliar woman answered, followed by the sheriff's wife, who came to see who was there. "Oh, you were sent by God!" she said. As it turns out, the sheriff's wife was pregnant and due at any minute. The family could not get the nurse they had engaged. "They knew that I had been a nurse, but not a baby nurse! But I had my uniform with me. Why and how, I do not know. It was absolutely unbelievable to me. Why did I even pack my uniform when I left the Mulders? This is Hashem that directs me."

She was immediately taken into the sheriff's home. Carla was shown a room where she could stay. "Everything was beautiful and clean."

Exhausted, Carla began to pray. "All I did was daven that the woman wouldn't have the baby that night. I begged Hashem to let me sleep that night so that I could recuperate from the ordeal of the walking." Carla quickly fell asleep.

The following night, she donned her nurse's uniform. The sheriff's wife gave birth around three o'clock that morning on February 4. Carla assisted the same doctor who had treated her while she was hiding at the Mulders. "Hashem was with me again because it was the same one that treated me at Pauline's. He did not show that he knew me." Around five or six in the morning, the doctor told Carla that he would return around ten in the morning to check on things.

> At that time, I began to feel ill. I broke out with blotches all over my legs and felt that I had fever. When the doctor returned, I asked if I could see him just before he left. We went in a small room, away from the baby, and I showed him my blotches. He said that I was very sick and there was no medication for my illness, erythema nodosum, an infection of the blood. He told me that it would take six weeks to clear up and be very painful And now when I look back, it was no wonder; I was so stressed out, and it has to go somewhere in the body. I was also incredibly underfed.

After the doctor diagnosed Carla's illness, the sheriff started to interrogate her. "The sheriff called me into his office. He wanted to know a little bit more about me. I don't remember exactly what he said, but he probably asked me where I had been. It was a totally strange business altogether. He had to protect himself. I got the feeling that the sheriff was trying to see what type of person I was. Who was I hanging around with? He could have said that I was a whore. I don't think we even saw the sheriff when I hid there the first time, when we only spent two days." Once Carla passed his test, he insisted that she stay with them. "Imagine. It is a big responsibility for him. I told him that I didn't want to stay there because I was sick and they had a newborn baby. I said to the sheriff that I heard that a hospital in Almelo was hiding people. I asked if I could go there."

Exhausted, Carla retreated to bed. Her sickness was very painful. Her legs were hurting terribly, covered with dark red blotches that were hot to the touch. She was suffering from a high fever. Carla knew that Pauline had once experienced the same symptoms. Carla knew this from one of their rare conversations in the Mulders' kitchen. Carla wondered if she actually got the illness directly from Pauline. However, she now realizes that stress must have been the underlying force in her deteriorating health. The doctor told Carla to remain in bed. "The family was fantastic. The minute the new mom could get up, she sat next to my bed. She said, 'don't worry, we are going to take care of you.'"

Once Carla had recuperated at the sheriff's, the doctor suggested that Carla go to the town of Hellendoorn where there was a sanitarium that treated patients with tuberculosis. She could have x-rays to make sure that she hadn't contracted tuberculosis as well. "They were afraid of TBC [tuberculosis]. So I went and had the x-rays done. It was very important. Who paid for this, I don't know. I didn't have tuberculosis, but the diagnosis instructed that I should not ever go out in the sun, like for sunbathing." Carla has no idea who organized or paid for the x-rays. For six weeks, Carla stayed with this family, whose name she'll never know. Finally, the sheriff told her that she needed to leave; it was too dangerous for her to stay with them. The sheriff found a young farm couple living down the road. They agreed to take her in. "These people did it to make money."

For the remainder of the World War II, a little less than four weeks, Carla stayed with the farm couple. They had a radio. That is how Carla heard that the war was officially over on May 5, 1945, via radio broadcast.

*One hundred seven thousand Dutch Jews were sent to camps.
About two thousand seven hundred fled Holland illegally.
One thousand left legally.*

In total, one hundred ten thousand seven hundred Jews left Holland, and nine hundred were eventually released from Westerbork. Total: one hundred eleven thousand five hundred.

One hundred forty thousand Jews lived in Holland before the war.

Twenty-eight thousand four hundred Jews survived.

Ten thousand Jews had been allowed to continue living there openly.

Eighteen thousand Jews, including four thousand five hundred children, survived by hiding until the war was over.[46]

Collecting Fragments

Carla came out of hiding on April 10, 1945, two and a half years after leaving Enschede. She was twenty-eight, a widow with no money or home, a mother who wanted her children. "On that day, the farmer told me that the war was over. He heard this on his radio. I left their farmhouse and walked directly to the Mulders because I wanted to get Jedidjah." Instead of returning her child, the Mulders began an interrogative conversation, asking Carla what she was going to do. She explained that she wanted Jedidjah and was going to head back to Enschede.

> And you know, when you are talking, you say something like, "Ah, as long as I have a bed to sleep in." *Do you know that they seriously offered me a bed in exchange for Jedidjah?* I said "No, thank you" to this exchange, of course. Can you imagine the philosophy after all this? *To give a bed instead of a child?* And then they said that they didn't even know if I was her mother. You can see that the woman was not all the way there.

The Mulders would not let Carla take Jedidjah. Carla became desperate and needed to act quickly. Clearly, she would need help to retrieve her daughter. "For some reason, I heard—and I don't know from where—but I heard that there was a young woman, Juliette Frankenhuis, who was hiding in the hamlet next to Marle." Carla left the Mulders, without her child, and headed for Juliette's.

Juliette, a familiar neighbor in Enschede and a member of the shul, was at least a link to her life before the war. Carla didn't know what else to do except go to Juliette and contact the organization. The family that hid Juliette welcomed Carla.

As soon as she could, Carla borrowed a bicycle with wooden wheels. "How did I get the bicycle? I don't know. People were willing to help one another. That's all I can tell you." The Germans had stolen all the rubber and used it in the war. Carla pedaled from Marle to Minister Overduin's house in Enschede, the head of the organization that hid her and her daughter. She was determined to get Jedidjah back. The Mulders told Minister Overduin that they couldn't return Didi because she was sick. They continued to give many different excuses for a long time. They constantly accused Carla of not being Jedidjah's mother.

After several weeks, two individuals from the organization went to Marle and convinced Pauline to give Jedidjah back to Carla, who at the time was still staying with Juliette.

> And of course, they reported this to me. This went on for over a month. So finally, they brought her back with just the clothes on her back. *Not even a clean pair of underwear.* She didn't even have her nightgown. Nothing. No clothes or any remnant of what she had while living with them. Jan and Pauline drove up in a car—maybe they borrowed it, or maybe it was a taxi—I don't remember. They just put her on the ground and drove away. They just dropped her off and left.

There she is. Can you imagine? What they told her before, I don't know. She is still messed up from that. We don't imagine such things happening at the time, but they did.

Upon Jedidjah's complicated return from the Mulders, Carla immediately discovered that Jedidjah's ears were racked with a serious infection that eventually required surgery on both. The procedure was done at the hospital in Enschede. "Her hearing is not the greatest on account of that." The idea of caring for a child in such a peculiar way still amazes Carla. She shakes her head in disbelief.

When your family, your home, your life are completely erased, rearranged, and spread out in hard-to-connect pieces, what does a person do "after a war"? No official The End sign scrolls across the sky. No one directs you to the nearest exit. According to Carla's practical side, one moves logically, one solid revolution at a time. In Carla's mind, the answer lay with collecting.

※※

For a second time, on a bicycle, with Jedidjah riding on the back, Carla pedaled her way from Juliette's in Marle to Enschede. She and her daughter needed a place to sleep and live. Since their home was at the Enschede shul before the war, it was the only logical place to return to after the war. "We went back to our home next to the shul and found that the de Vries family had also come back and had already moved in. I told them that I had nowhere else to go. They told me I could stay with them for a while."

Where was Channa?

After the war, Carla explains that hidden children would come home in different ways. If parents or family survived, they would find out where their children were through the underground organization or word of mouth. If parents found other familiar children in the same town or area, they would bring them home as well. Nothing was organized in this reunification of fragmented families.

Sometime near the end of May 1945, approximately six weeks after Carla came out of hiding; she made her way to the Thoomes family in Veenendaal. "For some reason or another, through somebody, I heard that the family where Channa had stayed wanted to meet me, but I can't remember if it was by telephone or a friend or another parent whose child had been in hiding too. They wanted to meet me because I had so meticulously packed her suitcase and the contents in it."

It took Carla a long time to get to Channa. Most of the bridges in Holland were destroyed. Cars, trucks, and bicycles were scarce. Carla eventually found partial transportation to Veenendaal on the back of a motorcycle. "With my winter coat and hat. I will never forget that."

Mr. Jan Thoomes was the principal of a high school in the town. "He and his wife, Ellie, were very nice people. They were very close with a Jewish family who came back after the war. Maybe they hid too. I don't know."

> I came to the Thoomses' home, and I saw my daughter. Through the front door, there was a foyer and then a hallway. I saw Channa down the hallway, and she came running down the hall toward me. I'll never forget that. She was almost a skeleton and six years old. It was terrible. Oh, she looked so bad.

The Thoomes explained that during the war they didn't have enough food. To Carla, their appearance was that of a well-fed and aristocratic family. "It wasn't in their makeup to go on a bicycle and try to get food in Eastern Holland. They had kept their maids throughout the war. But due to the lack of food, they had to send Channa to live with several families of the maids."

The experience of hiding took its heavy toll on Channa. She had poor vision, dysentery, and was extremely malnourished, though Carla was deeply touched by the family's sensitivity.

The Thoomes had friends who were observant Jews and therefore anticipated Carla's kosher dietary needs during the three-day visit. They arranged for her to eat with their Jewish friends.

> The Thoomes were very good-hearted people. They also hid two boys who were not Jewish, from Rotterdam, whose mother was sick and couldn't care for them all the time. They didn't have children of their own. After Channa left, Mrs. Thoomes became pregnant. They had, I think, three or four children. Again, this is a sign that they are good people.

Channa was two and a half years old when she was hidden. Carla remembers that before they separately went into hiding, Channa used to ask constantly, "'Where's my father?' I would maybe say, 'Your father isn't coming back.' But I didn't really know what to say. Or maybe I didn't say anything at all. You have to understand the circumstances." On their first night, reunited as mother and daughter, Carla and Channa slept closely together in one bed.

Channa asked only one question.

* *

At the beginning of the German occupation, May 1940, the Jewish population was approximately one hundred forty thousand, or 1.6 percent of the total Dutch population.
Anti-Jewish measures began in September 1941. Jews were first separated from the general population. Next, their property was plundered. Over one hundred million dollars of assets were extracted through various methods.
The first deportations began on April 29, 1942. It is estimated that one hundred seven thousand Dutch Jews were deported, of which only five thousand two hundred or 4.8 percent survived.
Between twenty-five to thirty thousand Jews went into hiding, assisted by the Dutch underground. Two-thirds of Dutch Jews in hiding managed to survive.
The last train left Westerbork for Auschwitz on September 3, 1944.
The geography of the Netherlands made escape difficult. The ruthless efficiency of the German administration and the willing cooperation of Dutch administrators and policemen doomed the Jews of the Netherlands. Less than twenty-five percent of Dutch Jewry survived the Holocaust.[47]

* *

Carla does not remember how she and Channa made their way back to Enschede. She thinks it may have been in the back of a truck.

Friends Philip and Juut de Groot survived the war by hiding and obtaining false identification papers. After the war, Philip had the task of exhuming the bodies of those Jews who were killed while in hiding. The victims were buried improperly either in a cemetery, yard, or field. Each of these individuals was due the respect of a suitable burial.

He was assigned to dig up the decayed bodies of those who were killed while being hidden. The congregation or partially of his own doing may have led him to do this. So he had to dig up these graves. I don't know how he did this. I don't know how many bodies there were. Apparently, he couldn't take it anymore; he went crazy. He committed suicide. It was about two or three months after the war. We just didn't talk about it. But I can still remember Juut standing there, getting the news. We were on a train to Assen. A friend told us that he was dead.

What is it like to "return" after a war? What do survivors say to each other? To others? Day-to-day details are vague. Of course, not everyone came back, leaving a void that continued to wound those who did.

From that time, I only remember that a few, like the de Vries, came back. Maybe if you saw someone you knew, they may have said, "I see you came back." People did not converse like they do here in America. Dutch people are not open. They are very introverted, much more reserved. You would not talk about anybody's business, personal feeling, or what your children were doing. Did people talk about hiding after the war? I don't remember, maybe once in a blue moon. I guess it was too painful. I guess people didn't want to touch the subject. After all, right after the war, how many people was I actually engaged with? I was close with my friend Juut. That's all. You know, it was a wonder that I found Juliette Frankenhuis! She wasn't a close friend, just a member of the shul. We didn't have much in common. She was a bubbly, outgoing person. I was much more reserved. She was nice enough to take me in. Andre officiated at her wedding, and her father-in-law was the shammes, *mohel*—

everything else in Enschede for many years. He survived.

So many important people in Carla's world were murdered by the despicable Nazi wrath. Philip de Groot survived the Nazis by hiding but could not escape their murderous aftermath. Carla's beloved cousin Ben-Zion and Renee Hirsch gave birth to twin girls on April 11, 1943. They were first sent to Kamp Westerbork and then deported to Theresienstadt.

When the war was over in Belgium and Holland, the Germans emptied the camps in a hurry and loaded all these people on trains. And they went all the way from Germany to Russia. Ben-Zion died on one of those cram-packed trains. He was the type of guy who would give the last crumb to somebody else. They put Renee and the twins, Betty-Shulamit and Nettie Yudith, in a camp by the Russian border. It was a dumping ground. The three all got typhus but survived. In 1946, when the twins were three, they returned to Holland. These twins were not looking more than a year old—no hair, very undernourished. What amazes me always is that they were so undernourished. If it is God's will, they would be healthy, and they were. It is unbelievable. Renee and I were very close. She brought them up very well. Today, Shulamit in Brooklyn has eight children, and Judith in Israel has seven. My cousin Renee was a very shy person. She came back to Amsterdam and got remarried to a Rabbi Eli Munk from England. She moved to London in Golders Green and raised the family. Rabbi Munk adopted the girls. He absolutely loved children. Eventually, the family moved to Israel. Rabbi Munk has passed away. Renee presently lives in Jerusalem. Some people can survive after the war and still be religious.

Leida Van Tyn married a childhood friend, Salo Boekbinder, whose father owned a department store in Assen. They lived in Holland a brief time after they married and then moved to France. There, Leida worked for Salo's uncle who owned a seed-and-potatoes business, Wolff and Son and Company.

During the war "Leida had blond hair, and Salo, he didn't really look Jewish either. I think in France they could walk on the streets. But at a certain point, they were betrayed. Salo was caught by the Germans. They didn't have any children. Leida came back in 1945 and started living with Mr. Boekbinder, Salo's father, taking care of his household. She eventually married a cousin of Salo, Ido Wolff, whom she later divorced."

Siegfrid Menko, president of the Enschede Synagogue's congregation, was murdered in Auschwitz.

Carla never heard the status of those involved in the underground organization. After the war she never had any contact with the volunteers who saved the lives of her and her daughters. She has no idea of how many people were involved or who they were. No way of saying thank you.

> I can see clearly what each one of them looked like. Of course, they never introduced themselves. That was not allowed. Too dangerous. What was the point? And remember, some came to Pauline's house, but I was not allowed to see them. Only once or twice did I get to speak with them; and that's when I asked for false identification, like Philip and Juut.

According to the Dutch Web site, De Joodsche Raad in Enschede, Minister Leendert Overduin, 1900-1976, saved over one thousand Jews during the war. He began hiding Jews after the Mauthausen razzia in September 1941—the same razzia that captured Andre—organizing one of the first resistance organizations in the Netherlands. The minister came from a liberal background and was an intensely inspired and driven human being, interested in helping his oppressed fellow man regardless of political persuasion, according to Gerrit Overduin, his nephew. In addition to saving one thousand Jews, he also found homes for children from the Dutch NSB after the war.[48] Minister Overduin also survived the war.

"I didn't find anything about my father, Joseph Nathans, until years later. He went to Auschwitz and was killed on July 7, 1942. He was fifty-eight. I don't know what happened to his second wife, Bep. The last letter I got from my father was from Westerbork."

According to Yad Vashem's Holocaust Martyrs' and Heroes' Remembrance Authority in Jerusalem, the Enschede Synagogue's assistant cantor—husband and father—Andre Andriesse, was murdered by the Nazis on October 14, 1941, at Mauthausen.

Bernard Schipper

Carla's life as a mother was slowly being pieced together. Both her daughters survived the war in hiding and were back again with her, living on the third floor of their former home, with the de Vries family.

The city of Enschede suffered greatly during the war. Prior to 1940, the city had a thriving Jewish community numbering two thousand. After the war, only a handful of Jews survived. The quaintly detailed architectural homes, buildings, and offices were bombed heavily. Because damage in Enschede was so severe and so many Jews did not come back, Carla recalls that a distribution of housing, goods, and basic necessities was organized by the city and the Jewish community for the handful who trickled back. Mrs. de Vries was responsible for the housing placement of the surviving Jews.

Carla's placement was to live in a few rooms in a large villa owned by the Serphos family, a mother and two daughters who also survived the war. Mrs. Serphos distributed nine available rooms, including an additional kitchen, to the different families who were assigned to her. Carla had a big living room, two bedrooms, and a small kitchen. "In the villa, Jedidjah and I shared a room. When we got Channa, she got the other room. Everything was a little mixed up, to say the least." Other occupants in the Serphos villa included Alfred and Reina Hen, who were not from Enschede but had hidden nearby during the war; and "two gentlemen," Bernard and Henry Schipper, brothers who occupied a room on the third floor.

Practically, how did these strangers, survivors of the war, manage to live together? Everyone contributed in the living arrangement based on his or her strengths.

> The request was that I was to cook for everyone. So I cooked on an iron stove with feet and a top, like a cast-iron stove. Because there was no coal to be had, a small canister burner was put on top of the opening of the stove. I put small sticks of wood in that and on top and made a small fire. The house had two kitchens. I had nothing to do with the owner's kitchen. Since the Nazis looted and stole all the food and resources, we had nothing to buy. No fabric for clothing, or even clothing, for that matter. No clothes. How I even got underwear, I don't know. We didn't have anything. Where you get linens from, I don't know. Towels, I don't know. The house was empty. There was no furniture because the Germans had stolen everything. But we all helped out and, somehow, became normal.

In response to the looting, the city assembled a furniture distribution center. There was a premium on beds. The mood was not that of stealing but carrying on. "You took the least amount of things that you needed. You didn't grab everything that you could possibly have. And for one reason or another, I found my dining room dresser and two chairs." Luckily, the brothers, Henry and Bernard Schipper, found a pushcart and were able to go back to the hall several times to collect furnishings for the home. "That impressed me. I didn't know these guys, and they were helping out."

Slowly, the new residents settled into a routine. This loosely assembled group first ate their meals together for at least two months. "However, when you have lots of people around the table, things can get busy. We had to split up at dinner and eat separately because I could not pay enough attention to my family." Henry Schipper and the other couple ate separately from Carla, Channa, Jedidjah, and Bernie Schipper. "It worked out very well for all parties. There was no animosity. We all liked each other, and it was all done with goodwill."

The dinnertime split-up was done mostly for Channa. "I didn't know her anymore." Returning to Enschede was not easy for her, and she was obviously unhappy. "I guess she felt forlorn or whatever it is. Jedidjah was already getting accustomed to the new living arrangements. I thought at first Channa might loosen up a bit and adjust to our new life. But she couldn't." Channa, six and a half, was confronted with a sister she had no recollection of knowing, a mother she had not seen for two and a half years, no father, and strangers, including a man named Bernard Schipper.

Carla refers to her husband as "Bernard." Everyone else calls him "Bernie." He is rotund with glassy blue eyes. His voice is high, and his hearing aid whistles. He does not hear it, but Carla and I do. A certain sweetness surrounds Bernie. Always a kippah on his head, he is a busy man. Leaving on errands with Walgreen's coupons in his hands or returning from a Talmud study session held in a meeting room at The Coves, Bernie is a cross-reference resource for Carla's sharp memory.

"Bernard, what is the mileage from Zwolle to Marle?"

"I think it is forty-three miles."

"Thank you, that's all." And then Bernie is officially excused. He returns to the kitchen, where he puts clean dishes from the dishwasher into the cupboard.

"I used to do that," Carla says, returning to the table. *Due to her illnesses and age, Carla's life has become physically limited.*

"*Now it is a whole different life. Bernie takes over, and he does everything. My life has so changed around. I made my own clothes and clothes for the children. I am just plain. I am not artistic. Some people have artistry in them. I like to do things with my hands. I love so to knit and crochet, cook, and bake.*"

Carla's and Bernie's relationship is symbiotic. Finishing each other's sentences is commonplace. Their fifty-year history is a constant rotation of dovetailed experiences. Throughout Carla's life after the war, her husband, Bernard Schipper, has been an equal partner at her side. "Bernie is an angel" is her constant comment. She says that his personality has blossomed over the years. "He used to be very shy. He was not someone in a company who would listen to jokes. Not him. But he has changed so much. If something fell off him from Germany, it might have to do with Jonathan. He has become more outgoing. My children saw this, too. It is just marvelous, for the better."

Bernie suffered horrendous losses in the Holocaust. His story of hiding, like Carla's, is chronicled through the Shoah Foundation. Once, during my many afternoons in the Schippers' home, Bernie sat with me, and we discussed his experience.

Bernie's parents were Polish citizens who came to Germany in 1913 where they became Germans citizens as well. "We might be called middle-class. There were very rich people in Braunschweig, with a cannery or department store, doctors, and lawyers. In comparison, my father owned a store that sold clothing, linens, and other stuff."

Until the age of fourteen, the children, Henry, Bernie and Paula Schipper attended public school. They were raised in an Orthodox home, and were active members of the Poale-Mizrahi Yisrael, an Orthodox youth group.

In 1933, because they were Jews, they were expelled from school. A cousin in Frankfurt told them of a *hachsharah* opening up dormitories for the Yeshiva of *Rav Breuer* (Rabbi Breuer). These hachsharahs were Zionist communities consisting of a few houses where Jewish youth lived and learned useful skills for living a productive life in Israel. The brothers applied and were accepted on scholarship. They attended until 1937 when the yeshiva's scholarships were cancelled.

Bernie tried to find employment by learning a trade. The Bavarian Jewish community in Munich opened a technical hachsharah to learn trades, and the brothers went there from 1937 to 1938. While in Munich, every fourth Shabbat, the Jewish community invited the students into their homes to have Shabbos dinner. On one of these occasions, the brothers were invited to the home of Victor Lowenstein, vice president of the Bavarian Central Bank. Bernie believes that sometime in 1938, Lowenstein was appointed to the Central Committee for Jews in Germany, an organization carefully organized by the Nazis to facilitate the German Jewish community to emigrate.

The Nazi threat was tightening its stranglehold. In Braunschweig in October, 1938, the police served the Schipper family a summons that ordered them to return to Poland immediately. Quickly, his parents called the Polish consulate in Berlin to find out what was going on. Bernie says that his parents were told that the Polish consulate had no information about the summons. They called their relatives in Hanover, Germany, and asked if they knew anything about the order to leave the country. Their cousins had not heard any such news. They spent the day frantically trying to figure out their best plan. At seven or eight o'clock that same evening, a Jewish friend came over to the Schippers' home and said that the Nazis were picking up Jewish men and women of Polish descent. Quickly, Bernie's mother grabbed some jewelry, and they fled by train to Hanover.

The Schippers arrived at the Hanover train station and called their relatives, who told them that the same thing was now happening there as well. The Schippers bought tickets, destined to go to Berlin where they felt they could be more anonymous.

Upon arriving in the morning, they telephoned another relative. "There, on Friday morning, we saw that they were picking up Jewish men only," Bernie says.

Bernie, Henry, and their mother stayed with their cousin while Bernie's father made his way around the city, trying to figure out the bureaucratic mess that was encircling their family. The Nazis were expelling the Jews by herding them on trains destined for Zobin, Poland. Since the Nazis did not have any record of Bernie's father for the roundup, he could work under the "radar." Eventually Bernie remembers that the roundup stopped.

The Schippers stayed in Berlin until Monday, and then returned home, except Bernie's father. "Where else could we go? When we came back, there was a seal on the door of our apartment. And so what do you do? My brother and I went to the police station, and there, by accident, we met the son-in-law of the landlord who owned the store that my father had rented. He asked what we wanted, and we said the door was sealed, and what do we do?" He took Bernie to his superior officer. The superior asked why they did not leave for Poland. "We said it was cancelled. We lied. He gave us the key back, and we went into the apartment."

Bernie's father, meanwhile, stayed in Berlin. He was desperately trying to figure out how to get the family out of Germany. He had a 1921 visa to get entry into the United States, but it was expired, issued only to him and useless. To escape, the Schippers needed endless amounts of paperwork, documentation, and birth certificates. A black market for such items, in addition to smuggling, was prevalent. Bernie's father was trying to get someplace, anyplace, in which to emigrate.

On November 9, 1938, Kristallnacht detonated Germany and a panic seized the Schipper family. Bernie's father was still in Berlin.

In Braunschweig that same morning, Gestapo officers, in civilian clothing, came to Bernie's home. "They asked us if they could come in. We refused to open the door." The door was made of a simple frame. A pane of decorative glass sat encased above it. The Gestapo officers broke into the Schipper home by smashing through the window.

> They wanted my father. He was in Berlin. But they took me in because I was the oldest. We walked in the street. Not too far from where we lived, there was a police substation, and I saw a policeman walking from there. As he approached us, I said, "Can they take me because I am a Polish citizen?" The policeman said no because I was under his jurisdiction. After a few hours of being held at the police station, I was taken to the Gestapo headquarters. They asked me why I was still here in Germany and not in Poland. And I gave them the same story. They said I had to stand at the wall with my face against it. The room was filled with piles of tefillin, prayer books, and all kinds of Jewish books. When I glanced at the piles, they punched me in the face. After a few hours, they told me to get out of Germany, or they would take me to a concentration camp. From there, I walked home.

After Bernie's confrontation with the Gestapo, the Schippers' attempts to get out of Germany were thrust into a desperate gear. Bernie said that rumors were mentioned about Cuban visas. But when his father followed this lead, they found nothing tangible. "You can get a visa to go to Shanghai. But who wants to go to Shanghai?" Bernie laughs. Bernie's sister was staying at a HaPoale Mizrahi hachsharah in Braunschweig. She came back and applied for a visa for either England or Denmark through HaPoale Mizrahi. She obtained a Danish visa and escaped. "We wanted her to go England but she wanted to go to Denmark. The reason: her future husband was there," explains Bernie. Meanwhile, Bernie's father's attempt to get out of Germany was failing. "My father couldn't find anything."

In the meantime, Mr. Lowenstein had moved from Munich to Berlin. Someone told the Schippers that Lowenstein might be able to help. Bernie went back to Berlin. "I don't know how I got the address and where I stayed there that day. All I know is that I found him, and I told him we needed visas. He said he'd see what he could do. A few days later, we got the visas to go to Holland through their association with the Poale Agudath Yisrael hachsharah."

On May 11, 1939, Bernard Schipper, nineteen, and his brother Henry, eighteen, came over the border to Holland from Germany. Bernard and Henry lived, along with twenty boys and four girls, in a villa situated on an incline, surrounded by small farms in the small village of Twekkelo, not far from Enschede and the German border. The leaders of the hachsharah group were Hillel and Malli Bruckenthal and their two boys. Bernie worked in Enschede in a factory that manufactured machinery for the textiles industry. The war started one year later, on May 10, 1940.

> On September 14, 1941, we got a phone call from the leader of the Jewish community that there was a razzia and we should disappear. This was the razzia that picked up Andre, Carla's husband. The Gestapo came with the NSB, the local police, but found only the girls at the house. On another occasion, we were also alerted by this same man. He had a textile family and connections with the local police. There was another one in May 1941 in reaction to the Dutch dockworkers' strike in Amsterdam for the treatment of the Jews.

Bernie remembers that in the spring of 1942, the Dutch Jews were ordered to wear the yellow star. Because of this government order, he and his brother decided to find work outside Enschede. Both found work on a farm. Bernie explains:

> So we had to wear the star. My brother heard that some of the boys got a notice that they should report

for work camp. The farmer that my brother worked for said that when you get the notice, don't go. We didn't get a notice, but a lot of boys did. In the fall of 1942, we got the notice that we had to register. We got our belongings that we had from the villa and brought it to the farmer, Bernard Koop, and he put these things in the barn.

The farm had two barns on its property. One was burned and abandoned. The other was newer and functioning. Bernie and Henry hid in the burned one for the next three years.

There was a new farmhouse because the old one burned out. But the old one was still standing with a room and an attic. So we got some beds up there. I don't know how we got these things up there. Two beds and two mattresses and blankets. With cardboard, we cordoned off around the beds and created some kind of living space. On top, we put some tarpaper because the roof was leaking. Then we went there. We gave the farmer what money we could. Everything was rationed then, and he eventually ran out. We were there a month, and we'd go back to the villa and check on things, even though there was a curfew. We wanted to know what was going on. We stayed from October 1942 to April 1, 1945. It was an April Fool's Day joke that we were liberated. The first Christmas was in 1942. Christmas evening, the farmer wanted us to come down in the house after their kids were sleeping. We found he had another Jewish couple in hiding in the new farmhouse. We didn't know them. They were from Enschede.

Bernard and Henry went into hiding on the Koop farm. The farmer and his wife had two children, ages eight and three. Bernard Koop's mother also lived with them. Bernie figures that the older child knew that people were hiding on the farm. He remembers hearing the younger child comment that she "heard something up above." The older sibling responded that the noises up in the barn were from the mice running around.

Bernie and Henry kept abreast of the war through the brave ingenuity of the farmer. "You were not allowed to have a radio. But the farmer had a radio in the new barn; I don't know how he got electricity out there into the barn. He'd listen to the BBC broadcasts and told us what was going on." To pass the endless hours, Bernie and Henry worked their minds.

> We took books, a series of books, about how to learn English, like Berlitz. They showed you how to read it but not how to pronounce it. One book by Robert Stevenson, *The Master of Ballantrae*, we read front to back and back to front; the characters were always engaged in smuggling. We were always reading. My brother had a dictionary he cross-referenced.

How did the brothers eat? What was their diet? "The farmer brought us coffee in the morning. I don't know what else he brought us. The warm meal was at mealtime; whatever they cooked, we ate too. We didn't eat any meat, and they knew that, although they used the same pots so you could still taste it a little bit."

Did Bernie and Henry know about the concentration camps and the Nazi plan to exterminate the European Jewry? "We knew about Westerbork. It was like an internment camp, similar to the Japanese camps in the United States. Westerbork was for illegals, Jews without visas. We knew that Jews had to go to work camps that existed before the war."

While Bernie and Henry hid with the Koops, their parents struggled to find a way out of Germany.

> They couldn't find anywhere to go. In Enschede, there was this man who had connections with German and Dutch smugglers. For two hundred and fifty guilders or about two hundred and fifty U.S. dollars, at the time a large sum of money, he'd arranged a way. He would bring my parents over from Germany to Holland and then to Belgium. I don't know how I got the money, but I paid him. There was already a black market, anyhow. They had two wooden boxes of belongings and those were smuggled, too.

In June or July of 1939, Bernie's parents attempted to escape from the Nazis across the Dutch-German border. They were to be picked up at the German border by a smuggler and headed through the forest. That night, with the brightness of the full moon, the German smuggler became spooked. He sent the Schippers ahead without him. They were told to look out for their pick-up person on the other side of the Dutch border. They walked through the dense forest, dappled with the bright light of the full moon, in the hopes of finding their Dutch smuggler and eluding the Nazis before the break of day. The first leg of their escape was successful.

During a summer morning, at six o'clock, someone walked into the hachsharah classroom where the boys slept, in the Twekkelo villa, asking for Bernie and Henry. The contact told them that their parents were at his farm and wanted to know what to do next.

> We said that someone would come and pick them up. We went to the contact man and explained to him where my parents were. He said that he would go get them. He did, and then they stayed at his house. That night he would take them to the Dutch-Belgium border. He took them to Brussels. They had an apartment there. In 1942, my father, while going to

> services in the morning, was picked up by the Nazis. We don't know where he went. There are no data... Auschwitz maybe. My mother was picked up a couple of months later. She was visiting some people, and they said that she should stay with them for the night. She insisted on going home to her apartment. They picked her up that night. The Belgium transit camp records and Auschwitz records from the Red Cross may show, but I don't know.

Bernie's sister survived. "After the war, my brother and I got a letter with the return address from "Schonewald" from Sweden..." I didn't know who that was. But it was my sister. She got married. In 1946, she and her husband went to Israel."

**

Carla vividly recalls her first meeting with Bernard Schipper.

> Before I moved into the Serphos' villa, I was sitting with Jedidjah on the patio at my home on Prinsestraat, next to the synagogue, and I saw two men walking up of the house. Seeing men this age at all was rare. They were dressed in suits and hats! I was very impressed, what can I say? I hadn't seen a man in so long. The two had come out of hiding in a farmhouse near Enschede in Twekkelo. They came to Enschede to see a girl who had also been in the hachsharah with them. She was staying now by the de Vries family, too. These brothers had somehow saved their clothing during hiding and were on their way to see Mrs. de Vries to help. Henry was the one who talked. Bernie never said a word. But I liked Bernie. Jedidjah defrosted him and she was very affectionate toward him right away.

Mrs. de Vries had assigned Carla, her daughters and the Schipper brothers to the same villa. Carla was appreciative for all the work the brothers did around the home. Jedidjah warmed up to Bernie immediately, crawling up on his lap and cuddling with him. She didn't make too much contact with her older sister, Channa, though. "And Channa didn't want to know anything from Bernie because she said that she had her own father."

Carla's interest in Bernie was mutual. "I was in love with Carla on account of the dress!" says Bernie laughing, referring to a soft green dress that they both remember. Their courtship moved at a quick clip.

In August, for her birthday, both Henry and Bernie gave Carla a vase that belonged to their mother. The couple went to the movies around the time of Queen Wilhelmina's birthday, a Dutch national holiday. A few weeks after their movie date, Mrs. de Vries asked Carla if she would take a job as a director of a children's home for children who came back from the war. "I asked Bernie's opinion, and he said that I should wait." Soon after that, the couple became committed.

After a few months, a house became available. Carla, the girls, and Bernie and Henry moved in. The home had a dining room, living room, a kitchen, three bedrooms, and a toilet. No hot water. No bathroom. "We got this house on the Borstelweg. It was better for the children to live privately in a smaller place. We had to go somewhere where we could get to know each other. I didn't know my children, and they didn't know me. Somehow or other we started living there. Bernie and Henry both got jobs because you cannot live by the air."

Carla ran the household and worked on her tailoring skills. Alfred Hen, who lived in the Serphos villa, was a tailor, and served as her mentor. "Realize that I didn't know these people from the birds while I was a nurse. Under his administration, I made a coat for Jedidjah that could stand on its own. He was a very good tailor. He took it a little too far. Alfred and

Reina had a son after the war, and they moved to Canada a couple of years before we came to America."

Bernie found employment in a toolmaker shop making band saws and safety equipment for machine shops. Bernie's brother Henry moved to Amsterdam in 1946. He lived in the PAI, the Poale Agudah house, and worked as a draftsman. From Amsterdam, he emigrated to the United States.

Life was beginning to revolve with certain optimism. Carla and Bernie decided to marry.

> We went to city hall to get the marriage certificate. The practice was to give cigars after the ceremony, but Bernie forgot the cigars, and we had to walk all the way back home to get them! I had an uncle, Abraham Nathans, one of five siblings on my father's side. He and his wife, my aunt Marianne, were the only ones to return back from the war. They were in Theresienstadt. They offered to have a *chuppah* in their house in Utrecht. We had to travel early from Enschede to Utrecht on a Sunday morning. It was so cold. So, we became kind of a family. It was nice for the children.

Carla, now remarried to Bernie Schipper, tried to establish a family and a life after the traumatic devastation of the war, a topic that no one found the words to discuss. In Enschede, the girls walked about ten or fifteen minutes to get to school. Next to the school lived two elderly sisters-in law, close friends of Carla and Bernie, whom they would visit, have juice with, and prattle with each day after school. "Tanta Hennie" and "Tanta Becky" were like substitute grandparents for Channa and the girls.

Tanta Becky's connection to Carla was threaded deeply. Tanta Becky was distantly related to Andre; her brother married a sister of Andre's third cousin. Although Andre's family tree is complicated to understand, the friendship between Carla, Bernie, and Becky would clearly be passed on to the next generation. This link to Andre is an important connection that continued to crop up in Carla's and Bernie's lives. During the war, Andre had family living in Indonesia who were incarcerated in a Japanese internment camp. After the war, the Frankens returned to Amsterdam and stayed with an uncle of Andre who survived, Braham Elzas. The Frankens eventually moved to Enschede. Louis Franken, who was about Channa's age, felt an inclination to become a more observant Jew, like his uncle Braham.

> Louis Franken's father was a fine, quiet individual. He, Bernie, and I clicked instantly. He told us about his son Louis who wanted to be more observant. Although they had a kosher home, they didn't observe as much as Louis would like. Louis was very impressed with Bernie, saying the prayers and laying teffilin. Louis would go to services alone and come home with Bernie and the girls to have Shabbos with us. Louis said "amen" at his own circumcision. He was like a son to us, and still is.

As a family, Carla and Bernie began to amass good friends. With the "Tantas," Louis Franken, the Hens, and many others, they began to build a loving supportive collection of individuals from the fragments that survived the war. Channa's distance from Bernie diminished slightly. She was, however, becoming an increasingly introverted girl and a voracious reader. Carla does not remember her having any close girlfriends in Enschede.

> She was not very verbal at all. She had suffered a lot, of course. After I got her back, she got sick. I am not sure of the illness. The doctor said she had to rest and stay in bed all the time. What is the reason? We never

knew. Later on we surmised that it might have to do with the thyroid. Reading was her only passion. That was about it. She was not a happy child. It was difficult for me to be with Channa. We did not have a close rapport or much conversation going on or many subjects to talk about. I honestly don't know if she was a happy child. And there was always a concern about Channa's health. I went to different doctors in Amsterdam to deal with Channa's eyes. She was cross-eyed. The eye problem was neglected and whatever was wrong was exacerbated on account of the war. I went to an eye institute in Utrecht when Channa was nine. I stayed there with my uncle and aunt, Abraham and Marianne Nathans, who came back from the camp Theresienstadt. Channa had surgery. It did not help. As a young adult in New York, she was diagnosed as being blind in one eye as a result of the neglect during the war.

Additionally, Carla was constantly sick. "What the problem was with me, I don't know. You have to realize what I went through all these years. Maybe it was gastrointestinal. Who knows?"

Tanta Ro Elzas, Andre's aunt, offered to help. She moved in and took over the housekeeping duties. Ro Elzas also hid during the war. The Nazis murdered all her children, including Carla's close friend Erna, who introduced Carla and Andre.

As the housekeeper, Tanta Ro ran a "tight ship."

I remember sitting at the kitchen table and Tanta Ro walked in. We were just sitting and talking. Jedidjah took one look at her and said, "When are you leaving?" I felt embarrassed, of course. The woman tried to help. I was always sick and upstairs in bed. When I felt I was good enough to come downstairs, we enjoyed the custom of sitting around the table and chatting after dinner. Tanta Ro would have none of that. When we finished a plate, it was gone! I told Bernie how much it bothered me. Bernie told me—and this is why I admire him—he said, "Do you think you can change a person that is already fifty years old?" He was so right. She eventually went her own way on good terms.

Carla's health was not improving. Someone suggested that she go to Switzerland to convalesce. Friends took in Jedidjah. Channa stayed with Tanta Becky in Enschede. Carla took a train to Switzerland and stayed with "friends of friends." "Crossing from Brussels to Belgium, I was searched through and through. The security is just as bad then as it is now. I had a tube of toothpaste that Bernie had put diamonds into; just in case I got into trouble, I could get some money. Carla went to recuperate with a Jewish family who lived in Zug, about a one-hour train ride from Zurich.

> They were polite but that's where it ended. It hit you in the head, their complete coldness. They were Jews, doing a mitzvah, and after the Holocaust they were, at the most, polite, and that's it. They'd go to the movies and leave me alone. For some reason, that gesture hurt me the most. I felt so terrible, like I was still in hiding. I made this difficult decision to leave Bernard and the children . . . it was terrible. I was supposed to stay for four weeks. But I couldn't stand it. I left after two. I came back to Enschede and got very sick again. I had fever and was sick. I had trouble in my mouth. It was a wisdom tooth. A dentist came to the house and into the bedroom and tried to pull out the tooth as I lay in bed. The whole experience was horrible.

The Mulders continued to play a role in Carla and Jedidjah's life. "They kept coming after her once she came out of hiding. They wanted to see her, wanted to be with her. We couldn't refuse that, but for her, it was a very difficult situation. These 'visits' went on for maybe a year. She was only three years old."

These visits were not easy for Carla as well. "Imagine, spending most of your first three years of your life with a loving couple that you see as your parents and then you are returned . . . to your mother. As a child, she had big trauma. Only since the last ten years has she straightened out."

From her time in hiding, one single photograph of Jedidjah exists. She is wearing a petite dress with tiny flower trimming, socks, and Mary Jane shoes. "She doesn't look happy," Carla remarks as she takes in the image.

After the hiding, once she became acclimated to life with Carla and Bernie, Jedidjah took on a tomboy personality.

> She gave us trouble but not anything really serious, but you know. For instance, I always had help in the house and Jedidjah had a skateboard. It needed repair because some of the metal was sticking out from it. We told her she was not allowed to use it because it was broken. But of course, she used it anyway while we were out of the house. Then, she fell and hurt herself and came in bleeding to the household help, a young girl who was pretty scared. She was always jealous of her older sister, Channa, as any younger sister would be. After all, Channa got to go to sleep later, and all these kinds of things.

In 1947, Carla was back at the doctor because she was not well. At that appointment, the doctor informed her that she was pregnant.

> I didn't know. When the doctor told me, I thought it was the happiest day in my life. I remember going back on the bicycle and coming home and telling

Bernie that we were going to have a baby. I had very easy pregnancies. I remember it was Tuesday, and I rode my bicycle to the fish market, and later in the day, I went into labor. I remember Bernie going to the bakery to use the phone at eleven at night to call the doctor. The thing was, in those years, you stayed home to have a baby. You didn't go to the hospital. But the doctor was in the next village and couldn't come right away. But he was there when Ruthie was born on August 5, 1947. I was bleeding profusely afterward. I had secured my friend Eva Saunders, a nurse, to help me after Ruthie was born. At first, she couldn't come because she was with another family. But then she came and stayed for about two weeks. Ruthie was a wonderful baby. So black! She had black hair all over her arms. It was unbelievable. It fell off after a while. We were told that if you are nursing, you are not to give a bottle to the child. With Channa, we were told not to feed the baby at night. That was the practice because the baby had to learn to sleep through the night. Somehow, they learn to do it. You kept the child in a different room with a nurse. But Bernie said that he was going to sneak a bottle to her anyway because "they all grow up!" She was a very easy baby. She was born mature and never gave us any problem, except the time she picked the flowers from the garden when she was three years old!

In 1949, a friend of Carla's and Bernie's told them that an Amsterdam businessman was looking for someone to take care of his business while he traveled. Bernie took the position and was later asked to be a partner. Although he could not afford the business proposition, he did commit to working in Amsterdam during the week, living with Carla's cousin Renee and her twins. He came home to Enschede for Shabbos. In

1950, Bernie and Carla decided that they should make the move to Amsterdam for Bernie's work.

> When we left Enschede, we had made several close friends who were difficult to leave. I talked about this with "Tanta Hennie." Her observations were very important to me. She was observant and knew how we would fare. It is so important to have someone like this in your life, and I knew this. She told me, "You are leaving good friends; that means you will find good friends wherever you go." Where I have gone in my life, I have seen how important it is to have friendships. Listen, I am an only child. I know how important it is. This gives you a description of my life.

After a year, the business began to decline. Bernie enrolled in an evening ORT course that taught typewriter and adding-machine repair; from there, he secured a position as a technician at an Underwood typewriter distributor. At that time in Holland, everyone worked a half of a day on Saturday. Carla told Bernie not to tell the boss that he could not work on Saturday but to suggest that he would work every lunch hour to compensate. The boss reluctantly agreed. "Everything is bashert," Carla says.

The girls were enrolled in the Rosh Pina Day School, but Jedidjah did not do well. "Academically, Jedidjah was a rebel. We had her tested for possible learning disabilities. The psychologist's prognosis was simple. 'She is like a butterfly. Don't worry about her,' they told us."

Of course, she made it through the school and went to high school in America. Jedidjah was fine, with lots of friends."

Bernie had a steady job. Carla was sewing. "I made all my own clothes and those for my daughters. I had made a beige brown coat and hat for Ruthie. She was always running late to kindergarten not too far from where we lived. We lived on the third floor with a small window that you could open up, and we'd watch her. We joked that she always looked like a meatball, rolling to school. She was so cute."

Life in Amsterdam was very social with lots of friends and gatherings. Although the family struggled with finances, they managed piano lessons, private Hebrew education, countless medical procedures, and, eventually, emigration to America. Carla shakes her head when she reflects on how she and Bernie made all those things happen. The couple had established a family life that was enveloped by a large circle of friends.

> We had several friends. One family we knew before the war: Hanna, from Het Apeldoornsche Bosch, and Jaap Brilleman. They had a little boy, Jehudah. He was a biter. I can still see him in the high chair. They moved to Israel after we moved to America. We were also close with Hanna and Mendel Jeret. They had three children. They made aliyah. We were close with Emil Mendelson. He no longer had his friends or family, so we were like family to him. He would spend the night and sleep in front of our *haart*. Life was so nice in Holland. Tetta even came to visit. We always had friends and visitors. That was my household.

But soon, Carla would be uprooted again. This time the danger was the Soviet Union. "After World War II, Holland began to feel threatened by Russia. We didn't want to be in the same trap as with Germany."

Hidden Years

In 1951, Carla and Bernie mulled over the idea of moving to America. The family knew how to speak English, but that is where their knowledge of life in the States ended. The imposing weight of the Soviet Union outweighed the benefits of staying in the Netherlands.

Bernie's uncle Max and brother Henry were already in America. Uncle Max Schipper was in the scrap metal and rags business. Henry was a salesman for Fuller Brush Company in New York and had opened an appliance store. Uncle Max's wife Fanny used to send care packages to the girls in Amsterdam. The contents were usually clothes and shoes. Carla laughs as she recalls these contents of the packages. "The shoes were terrible, so ugly. We made the girls wear them anyway, and they never forgave us for that! We were appreciative, don't get me wrong, but those shoes were so bad."

Bernie asked his uncle Max to give an affidavit for the family, therefore expediting the emigration process. Max said he would only give an affidavit for Bernie, not Carla or the girls. Carla contemplates the rejection with a long pause. "My husband didn't want to leave me alone, so consequently he didn't go."

However, two years later, on November 11, 1953, by their own will, the Schippers did come to the United States. Ruthie was three years old, Jedidjah was eleven, and Channa was thirteen when the family arrived through the Port of Hoboken on Veterans' Day.

"We had to schlep our stuff off the boat. No one was working because it was a holiday," says Carla. "We came to Henry's house, and I met my sister-in-law, Rose, for the first time." There, the family temporarily moved in with Bernie's brother's family, Henry and Rose. They had one child and were expecting a second. Bernie and Carla added five more. The apartment, cramped at best, was on Ft. Washington Avenue. The situation was tense.

"Henry's family did not have a towel by their kitchen sink, so we had to use the paper towels. I decided the next day to replenish the paper towels that they used. After all, we were an entire additional family that was living in Henry's home. This gesture deeply offended Rose. I overheard her saying that the Dutch people are very stingy, cheap, and miserly."

Carla felt bad. "She did not take it the way I intended. She was offended. I didn't know to go out and buy a plant or something. Don't forget, we came with five people. I didn't mean it that way. I wanted to please her."

Determined to make a strong start in America, Carla and Bernie rode the subway downtown the day after they arrived and obtained Social Security numbers. "We had never *seen* or been on a subway before in our lives." Bernie found a job within days as a mechanic at American Business Machines at 573 Broadway.

After one week, and probably to Rose's great relief, the Schippers took up their own residence on the first floor of 390 Wadsworth Avenue in Washington Heights. "We found a professional apartment," explains Carla. "The type you rent out to a business."

Their furniture arrived a few days after they moved in. Carla says that although the girls were not happy about being uprooted again, they adjusted socially to their new surroundings through the *Agudah* organization.

America was a whole new experience for the children. Henry had a store at 164 Broadway where he sold household appliances and a new product. Television. Henry and Rose had one in their home. "My children, for the first time, saw a television. They watched *Howdy Doody*. We couldn't get them away from the television! They were so enthralled."

American culture was a shocker for Bernie and Carla as well. While sitting with a friend of Henry's in a coffee shop, they were served overflowing cups of the hot brew. Carla and Bernie were shocked. "In Holland, you would never have a cup all the way filled. It was like something the farmers would do. It was dirty."

Carla's sewing skills would now be a financial asset to the family. "In Amsterdam, I asked my cousin Renee if I could make clothes for her children so I could hone my sewing skills. I couldn't just depend on Bernie. I can still see the dresses in front of me that I made for the twins Judith and Shulamit."

Carla hung a sign in the apartment window that simply said "Alterations."

"I got some customers on account of that." One such customer was a Mrs. Lamm, who lived at 382 Wadsworth. "As it turns out, Mrs. Lamm explained that she has a cousin by the name of Lina Elzas. Thereupon, I say, that was the aunt of my husband Andre! We became close immediately. It was such a wonderful feeling!"

Bernie earned sixty dollars a month. Even though Carla was making money from her sewing, meeting the ninety-dollar monthly rent payment was difficult. They lived a very frugal life. Carla was always looking for extra income. In November 1954, the family secured a less-expensive apartment on the second floor of their same building. Carla cultivated a steady stream of customers, doing mostly hems and sleeves. But once summer arrived, the customers headed for the Catskills. A "seamstress wanted" ad in the classifieds of the *Aufbau*, a German Jewish newspaper, attracted Carla's attention.

> I went to the address on Madison Avenue. It was very fancy. The owners were Jewish. These people were real rotten Germans. They treated me horribly. I didn't know the exact German terminology right away for a dart, hem, buttonhole—all the alteration terms. After a week, I was walking on my break and I started crying. I talked to my father, 'You didn't bring me up to be like this, so miserable.' I went back in after my break and told them that I quit.

As a seamstress, Carla frequented the Sach's Notions Shop in Washington Heights. "It was a nice Jewish store. I asked the owner if he had any work. He said he had a client of his that may be interested. It was Thursday or Friday. I telephoned this person on Sunday. Her name was Inge Adler. She asked me to come over right away. She was a freelance sample maker for material manufacturers. We hit it off right away."

Inge and Carla arranged a work schedule so Carla could be home by one o'clock in the afternoon for Ruthie, who was in first grade. Carla was able to contribute to the family income and be home for her youngest child. Her skills as a seamstress improved further under the skillful eye of Inge.

"Although I often took work home with me, I was always there when the girls returned from school. At four thirty, Channa would come and ask me what I wanted her to make for supper. I would already have the meat prepared, but she would make the potato and the vegetable. I was still busy sewing." This arrangement lasted for many years.

The girls each adjusted differently to their lives in the United States. In January 1957, they welcomed their younger brother Jonathan into the family. Each daughter recalls that they were happy to have a little brother in their family. Neither Carla nor her daughters mention that the span of time—ten years difference—between Ruthie, the youngest, and Jonathan served as a cause for stress or awkwardness.

But Jonathan was no ordinary brother. His needs obviously went beyond that of a newborn. With an unclear diagnosis, and Carla and Bernie determined to seek out his best potential, attention to the other three girls had to be divided.

The family had established a fine-tuned routine. Carla and Bernie both worked. The girls ran the household, assisting in preparation of meals, picking Jonathan up from school, and doing other chores. All the daughters agree in their admiration for their parents' efforts to pursue a new life as a family and forge new ground for their brother. Congruently, the siblings appear to revolve in their own separate worlds.

Each daughter matured during the late 1950s and early 1960s on completely individual paths. From Carla's perspective, Channa was a rather private and introverted individual. Their mother-daughter relationship was distant. Their history, fragmented by the war, never firmly came together. Channa did not want to leave Amsterdam. Socially a quiet child in Amsterdam, she had finally made close friends. Leaving was painful.

As an adolescent in the United States, she never really connected with her peers. After high school, Channa chose not to go to college but to work in order to save up enough money to go back to Amsterdam. Eventually, she sailed back to Holland; and in Amsterdam she took up residence in religious dormitory-style housing, working for a Jewish community social agency.

But Channa began to have questions about her religion during her adolescence. As a young adult, she felt the conventions of Orthodox Judaism were stifling. She returned to the United States looking to either branch out or fit in.

Upon returning to the United States, Carla and Bernie rented a room for Channa in the house next door. After a couple of months, Channa found an apartment in midtown. She shared the space with Varda Gross and another girl. By this time, in 1960, Channa, twenty-one, was an independent young woman. Music was an anchor in all her routes of interest. She began to teach choral groups. She participated in civil rights marches. She tried spiritual awareness through Unity and yoga. Channa's exploration of the world outside her traditional Jewish lifestyle coincidentally led her younger sister Jedidjah to Michah Gross. "Channa's roommate, Varda, had a younger brother," Carla explains. "This is how Jedidjah came to meet Michah." They began dating in 1962.

> My daughter had a difficult time because Michah's mother didn't like her. The father, Abrahm Gross, came to see us to inspect how many books we had and what kind. He looked us over. He looked for the Gemara, which is a sign to frum people that a certain level of religious observance is being obtained in the household. We did not have a set because we were not so frum that we needed to have it in the house. Michah's father announced that Michah was too young and shouldn't get married yet. He told Bernie that he was a *Kohayn*. So Bernie said to him that his mother was a daughter of a Kohayn. That's important because Kohaynim represented a certain status. For the wedding—which took place on January 27, 1963, a Sunday afternoon—the family arrived late on Friday due to bad weather. The women were crying because it was after sundown, and they couldn't light the Shabbos candles. You can imagine the mood around the dinner table that night. How involved were we in this relationship that our daughter had chosen? These types of life decisions we left up to our children; after all, it was their life. Like I said, we never really put our stamps

on the children. I think we had too much on our mind with Jonathan. And we are not that way, anyway. From January to August of 1963, Michah and Jedidjah lived close by in an apartment in Washington Heights.

The young couple rented a basement apartment in Waterbury where Jedidjah's bridal gown, handmade by Carla, and silver candlesticks, precious wedding presents, were stolen. In October 1966, their first child, a daughter, Tanya was born. Their first son, Ashi was born in 1968. In 1971, the family moved to Israel.

Ruthie attended public school in New York because Carla and Bernie could not afford a yeshiva education. However when she entered the sixth grade, both felt she needed more Jewish education. She received tutoring and began her studies at the Breuer Yeshiva.

"Financially, somehow, we managed to do it." The Schippers became industrious members of America's thriving middle class.

In 1963, soon after Jedidjah's wedding, Bernie became ill with the flu. While he was home, he asked Carla to bring some paperwork back to the office. David Silver, Bernie's boss at American Business Machines, knew that the Schippers had four children. It was not until Jedidjah got married, when Jonathan was six years old, that the Silvers discovered that Jonathan had Down syndrome. "We were not the kind of people who would talk about that. There was no reason."

While at ABM, Faye Silver, David's wife, told Carla that she needed someone just like her to work there. "I told her, 'How can I work here when you know what I have at home?'" But Faye was insistent, telling Carla, "You have so many friends. Surely, they can come in your home and watch Jonathan for a few hours." Carla knew that the extra income would help. She went home and discussed the idea with Bernie, who spoke with David Silver. "He told Bernie that they'd love to have me if Bernie could handle having me at work with him!"

Carla found a babysitter to take care of Jonathan while she worked part time five days a week. Her job responsibilities were mostly related to bookkeeping. "The second day, I am scared like hell. So the boss said 'How are you doing?' I gave him a look of frustration, and he pointed to the eraser at the end of my pencil. He said, 'Do you know what this is?' Implying that if you make a mistake, it is not a big deal."

The other women in the office began to take advantage of the "new girl," passing off busywork and extra work to Carla.

> I got sick of the fact I was doing a lot of things that were dropped in my lap and the girls were not doing anything. After two and a half years, I made up my mind that I wanted to leave. Years later, Jonathan had established that he was afraid of heights. He connected this with a fall down the stairs while being watched by the baby-sitter while I worked at ABM. He was not good at expressing his thoughts at the time, but years later we discussed this.

After a short stint with a curtains wholesale business, Carla found her niche with Behrman House Publishers.

> I presented myself on Thursday or Friday and was hired. The mother of my sister-in-law passed away over the weekend. I called on Monday morning and said that I am very sorry, but I have a funeral. They said not to worry about it, to come when I can! The place was fantastic. Places like this don't exist anymore. They didn't exist then! First, I worked on a machine that was like the forerunner to the Excel program. It was difficult, but I learned. After a while, I did regular bookkeeping. The boss, Jacob Behrman, saw me working on the calculator and always looking at the numbers. He came by and put his hand on my

hand and told me that I could do it without looking at the numbers. And I did. If it was lunchtime, everyone ate together around a conference table. Mr. Behrman used to come with a box of cookies and cakes ... It was so genial. Editor Andrew Amsel and manager Jack Roth were so great. It was a great job, absolutely fantastic.

**

In September 1941, Carla watched her first husband Andre be rounded up by the Nazis and marched away from her life. Her father, countless family, and friends were murdered in the Holocaust. Her life swiftly tumbled into a mental and physical nightmare of anguish, hiding, and outrunning the Nazi murderers. However, no mention of these events was discussed in her home after the war. "The minute we moved to the United States, our past was basically erased. It was as if it didn't exist. It was always lurking but never confronted," says her daughter Jedidjah Gross. However, Carla does not see the lack of conversation as deliberate.

> We never talked about the Holocaust. This was not on purpose. That might have been a mistake. We went through so much but we never talked about it with the children. They were very young, still, after the war. We were living life. Other things came up. We were both happy. We were living a normal life. We are not the type of people to talk about it. We didn't see it as a necessity.

The void of dialogue was, nonetheless, a presence in Carla's life. Her elder daughters Channa and Jedidjah both reacted to their experiences in opposite ways—one embracing Judaism, and the other fleeing it. Layered upon these reactions are the complexities of remarriage, immigration, and two more children, one with Down syndrome. Channa and Jedidjah tightly suitcased shut their own thoughts and feelings about their distorted early childhood as they began yet again another new life, this time, in America. Nothing about the past was discussed.

Channa dealt very privately with the loss of her father. Jedidjah rendered herself as a rebel. And Ruthie, born after the war, does not appear to carry any psychological baggage. Jonathan has very little grasp of a topic that is incomprehensible, no matter the intellectual capacity.

Throughout Carla's life, her coping is balanced on her solid fulcrum of faith. Devotion to her religion nourishes her positive perspective on life. Anyone who knows Carla is familiar with her warm optimism. Holocaust educator and scholar John Iorii explains, "So many people I know that go through this have no belief in God. None." Iorii has interviewed and videotaped survivors' stories since the early 1980s. He met Carla and Bernie through word of mouth. Both have spoken to students in his intense Holocaust Studies class at Episcopal High School in Jacksonville, Florida, most recently in September 2004. John says that there are only a "handful" of survivors left in the area. He tries to reach his students by making the generation-to-generation, survivor-to-student connection in the classroom. "Her devotion to God is firm."

Carla, throughout her eighty-seven years, has never questioned her Judaism. She approaches each day with strength, charisma, and moxie—traits that truly define a survivor.

A Fair Chance

*I*n October 2004, I e-mailed a gentleman in Israel, Herb Greenberg. I know from my interviews with Carla that Herb Greenberg and his wife, Barbara, are important people in Carla's and Bernie's life. I asked Mr. Greenberg if he would like to assist me in my research of Down syndrome, the Schippers, and the Holocaust.

The next time I met with Carla, she mildly chided me for not letting her know that I contacted this man. "You know," she says, sipping her tea and smoothing the plastic cover over her tablecloth, "You didn't tell me you'd be contacting Mr. Greenberg." I looked at her and felt as if two strong hands were squeezing my shoulders. I instantly broke out in my usual hot sweat (I've never had a cold one). I asked myself, "Who exactly is in charge here?" And then I felt the heavy squeeze again. This process was to be orchestrated by Carla's conducting, not mine. The weight released. I apologized for the faux pas. She brushed it off with a laugh. I made a mental note to always ask permission to gain entrance into her world. We began to talk.

Herb Greenberg has met thousands of parents and children. He is a respected and eminent educator with a focus on Jewish children, special needs children, and is the founder of the Tikvah program at Camp Ramah in Palmer, Massachusetts, part of the Conservative Jewish Movement's worldwide summer camp program.

Both he and his wife, Barbara, have commanding curriculum vitae in the field of education. They are also very close friends with Carla and Bernie, coming together through the nexus of Jonathan. They possess a deep respect for the Schippers because of their shared history with Jonathan. Mr. Greenberg explains:

> Though both Carla and Bernie suffered grievous family losses during the Holocaust, they both remained resolute in their commitments to the Jewish tradition. They are a couple that never accepted the status quo. After reclaiming their freedom as well as their surviving children after the war, they set about to rebuild a Jewish home in America. The birth of Jonathan represented a blessing to them, and it sent a clear message to the Nazi purveyors of hate and genocide that they could not destroy the Jewish tradition of commitments to the preservation of all God's creations. The Jewish principle of *tikum olam*, repair of the world, aptly applies to the Schippers.

The resolute determination to find a proper upbringing for their son is exactly what one would expect from someone like Carla.

After Jonathan was born in 1957, a parade of psychologists, surgeons, and good and bad teachers marched through Jonathan's childhood. "It was very expensive. How we paid for it, I don't know. These are miracles. I really don't know," says Carla.

Jonathan was not to be institutionalized. He was not to be pitied. He was to be given the opportunity to engage in life. According to Greenberg, "The public consciousness began to be catalyzed in the 1960s through the efforts of President Kennedy and his family, who shared with the American people details about his mentally retarded sister." America's awareness of Jonathan's developmental needs was about a decade premature. The country's collective awakening of the potential and special needs of the Down-syndrome community would gain momentum in the 1970s. The Schippers could not wait for society to wake up. They decided to be the alarm clock for their son.

By 1960, when Jonathan was three years old, Carla and Bernie took him to see Dr. A. Kameny, a speech pathologist. He and Jonathan formed a positive relationship which Carla attributes to Jonathan's successes.

> Dr. Kameny was tremendously impressed with Jonathan. He knew that Jonathan had potential. When he was still in the baby carriage, he had an instinct. He could tell if people were sincere or not. He could feel it on the people. He knew exactly how to treat people who didn't believe in him. While living in New York, there was a lady in the street whom I didn't know. I was with Jonathan, who was in the stroller. Somehow, she was nice to him in a different way, not a feeling-sorry way. Jonathan, at this early age, noticed this. Also, at two and a half years old, Jonathan was already potty trained. He kind of trained himself. This was not typical of Down-syndrome kids. As a young child, Jonathan wasn't much of a talker. Dr. Kameny encouraged him to be more outgoing by using a variety of methods. Some worked. Some didn't. For instance, he recommended that in the summer we should go somewhere there were small children so Jonathan could socialize. We went to the Catskills for four weeks at a small vacation community. But it didn't help. There

was not much communication between Jonathan and the other kids. For me, it was terrible. I hated it. I mean, I didn't mind it, but we were strangers.

The Schippers returned from the Catskills and tried another of Dr. Kameny's suggestions: mainstream education. "'Try to get him in a setting with normal children,' he says." Jonathan was four years old at the time. Carla recalls turning to the Help and Reconstruction Agency, a social service agency that aided German Jews and other Jews. The organization had a school and nursery with Jewish children and teachers. "We enrolled Jonathan in this program, and he did very well there."

> While sitting in a bus one day, when Jonathan was about four and a half, he says "Look, GE," pointing to a General Electric billboard. I was stunned. I thought, "How does he do that? Maybe he can learn how to read." I had a friend that was a teacher at the Breuer Yeshiva in New York. She was teaching elementary school. I said to her, "I would like for you to try to see if Jonathan could learn to read." So she came to my house with a primer and says, "Do it yourself." This was not done in a maligning way. She was afraid it wouldn't work, and it was our friendship at stake. I tell you, he picked it up in no time flat. He practically taught himself to read. Maybe the television had something to do with it, I don't know.

When Jonathan was about five years old, in 1962, it was time for him to start his elementary education. "We went to different schools and found a public school with a special education program and enrolled him there. It was a half-day program with about ten to fourteen children in the class of a mishmash of ages. The teacher looked older than I look now." The experience was one of many that would turn sour. "In 1964 I had some not-so-serious surgery and had to stay in bed for a couple of days." While Carla was recuperating, she noticed that Jonathan's behavior was becoming peculiar. "He didn't feel like dressing himself in the morning, which is not like him," she explains. "I am a person who finds a reason for things. I usually meet the teacher and get acquainted. But I couldn't because I was in bed, recuperating." Carla explained her concerns to her daughter Ruthie, who, at the time, was bringing him to school and picking him up while Carla convalesced. Upon returning home from school with Jonathan, she told her mother that the teacher was placing Jonathan in a baby carriage. "So that explains that," says Carla.

At five and a half years old, Jonathan was back at home. "I was never approached by the school about why we kept him home. He watched a lot of television," Carla flatly states. "When Jonathan was between schools, there was nothing else to do. Sure, there were lots of schools, but practically none of them were interested in having a Down-syndrome child in their school. This was a big problem."

Finding an appropriate enriching educational experience for Jonathan was a never-ending, expensive, and exhaustive search. In addition, the rent needed to be paid, and two incomes were needed. Carla managed to juggle work and her quest of decent education for her son.

Carla and Bernie found the Adams School, a private school, for Jonathan in Manhattan, a short distance from Behrman House. The tuition was a pricey two thousand five hundred dollars in annual tuition. Jonathan attended, as a first grader, in 1965. His class was small, comprised of only five or six children. He alone could read. Carla explains that because of this, it was easy for the teacher to give him a book and let him go. But Jonathan was with a teacher who cared for him, and he flourished in this setting. Unfortunately, his second-grade experience fizzled. He and his second-grade teacher were not compatible.

> His way of showing distress or frustration always had a pattern. He showed it by not getting dressed or feeling sick or not wanting to go somewhere. He ended up sick with pneumonia right after a little time after school started. He was home for at least two months. We never heard from the school except to pay. We explained that he couldn't go, but we had to pay anyway. It was about two hundred dollars a month. It was a lot of money. But they kept sending the bill.

Then Carla received a telephone call from Jonathan's beloved first-grade teacher from the Adams School. "She took a professional risk by calling me directly," explains Carla. The teacher told her that it was important for Carla to place Jonathan back in the first grade with her. She noticed how much Jonathan disliked his present teacher. "And all this time, I never heard from the director about this issue."

The Schippers requested that Jonathan be moved back to the first grade with his favored teacher. In addition to taking notice of Jonathan's educational needs, the teacher was well aware of the high costs of educating such a child. Having experience teaching in Westchester County, she suggested to the Schippers that they consider moving somewhere in Westchester County so he could enroll in the school district's special-education program.

Jonathan was nine. He was reading. This teacher felt, like Dr. Kameny, that he could be mainstreamed. The Schippers decided to explore the idea of moving.

They first consulted with Rabbi Philip Weinburger of Anshei Shalom in New Rochelle. Carla and Bernie also met with the head of the Westchester County Special Education Department and the district's psychologist. "The majority of children with Down syndrome were classified as uneducable, and teachers and educators largely ignored the field of mental handicap. Parents were also told that there was little that could be done to alleviate the effects of the mental disability. Many accepted this and often provided the child with less stimulation and activity than ordinary children."[49] The district offered two types of curriculum: trainable or educational.

> Of course the psychologist felt that he should be in the trainable tract, but we knew that Jonathan was educable. I told her that I was sorry to disagree, but he belonged in the educable program. The trainable was for the low functioning, and the educational is for those to go higher. The psychologist balked. So I made a proposition and told her to put him in the educable for the first three months and if he doesn't work, pull him out... I was right.

In 1966, banking on the potential of the special-education program, the Schippers decided to take Jonathan out of the Adams School and make the move to New Rochelle. Carla, Bernie, Jonathan, nine years old, and Ruthie, nineteen, moved to an apartment that was a reasonable twenty-minute walk to their new shul and railroad station. Carla had to give up her job at Behrman House.

Financially, the situation remained tight. Carla became a bookkeeper for a "stingy" accountant who owned several gasoline stations. "After five years and only receiving a five-cent an hour raise, I quit. But I learned a lot because in every job you learn something." She then found a quality position as assistant bookkeeper with an importer/exporter, Kane International, Inc. There, she flourished professionally until she retired.

While the family lived in New Rochelle, Ruthie graduated from nursing school at New Rochelle Hospital. Immediately, she began to look for a job as an operating-room nurse and was hired at Columbia Presbyterian Hospital. She married Abraham Jacob "Yankee" Goldstein in 1973.

The New Rochelle move would garner mixed reviews. "Jonathan didn't learn very much, but okay."

Educating Jonathan

Jonathan's elementary school education was filled with stops and starts. Although he did not have friends or teachers who understood him, he did have his parents' fortitude that carried him through the educational system. "Carla and Bernie were prime 'movers and shakers' in the public schools," explains Greenberg, familiar with the couple's high expectations for Jonathan while at Camp Ramah. "They often chided teachers and administrators for not adopting more challenging approaches for working with youngsters with Down syndrome."

By the time Jonathan was ready for high school, Carla and Bernie did not feel high school was adequately equipped for Jonathan. They chose to keep him in junior high, which had its drawbacks. Boredom with Jonathan always led to problems. Carla knew that keeping Jonathan engaged and challenged was tantamount. She decided to develop an afternoon activity program. "The Schippers' efforts often produced positive results for all developmentally challenged youngsters in their community. Carla organized after-school programs to enable Jonathan to pursue many of his creative interests. Jonathan, for example, became quite adept at sewing designs on pillows, and learned how to use a computer," said Greenberg.

> I thought that they shouldn't sit in front of the television after school, so my friend and I went to the New Rochelle Catholic College and asked for a classroom to use. We found a teacher that did silk-screening. We wanted them to do something with their hands. We made a creative curriculum for their children. This included making Christmas cards in order to teach them about basic economics. We invited the parents so they could buy the cards and the children could make a profit. This went on for about two years.

Carla's intense involvement finally paid off. She found a great special-education program in nearby Mamaroneck High School. "The teacher, Mrs. Friedman, she was terrific. He learned more from her than all the years of his life." Jonathan stayed at Mamaroneck with Mrs. Friedman until he earned his high school diploma.

Jonathan was being raised as an observant Jew. "All my children could *bensch* from five years old. I am not bragging, just explaining that this is the kind of life we have." By twelve years old, he had already learned several of the blessings necessary for his bar mitzvah. This full-throttle upbringing and set of expectations that Carla and Bernie employed was a rare way of parenting the Down-syndrome child of the 1960s and 1970s. "Carla and Bernie created a new identity for Jonathan, a Jewish identity, which had a profound effect upon his emotional, social, and linguistic development. Jonathan was provided with a rich Jewish education in his home, a program not offered at the time in the Jewish community," explains Greenberg.

To further enhance Jonathan's Jewish education, Carla and Bernie searched for a *Talmud Torah* program. He began at Young Israel Shul in New Rochelle.

Again, Carla, Bernie, and Jonathan faced the obstacles of an inexperienced teaching mentality in regard to the Down-syndrome child. Although Jonathan always attended classes, the instructor claimed that he was gaining nothing because he didn't participate. Carla and Bernie disagreed. "He came home and repeated everything he was taught. So we decided to have him tested, one on one. One day, when the class was on the playground, a Mr. Weiderhorn asked him some questions, and he did very well."

Undoubtedly, he was learning. His weakness lay in the fact that he was not participating on a level similar with the other students. It was clear that Jonathan was perfectly capable of learning the Talmud Torah curriculum, and one-on-one instruction was needed. Carla and Bernie decided that Jonathan would do better in a more personal setting and asked Mr. Weiderhorn to tutor him. Carla credits Mr. Weiderhorn with teaching Jonathan *layning*, learning to chant Torah and haftarah. Jonathan was given a rare Talmud Torah classroom opportunity when he was invited to attend another Torah class that instructed students in the proper haftarah blessing. "Rabbi Weinberger of Anshei Shalom suggested that Jonathan attend the class, and we grabbed it."

In addition to the Talmud Torah class and Mr. Weiderhorn's tutoring classes, Jonathan was supported by yet another individual, who believed he was capable of learning the practice of Hebrew prayer: Bezalel Shandelman.

When the Schippers first arrived in the United States in 1953, living on Wadsworth Avenue, Carla did her daily errands on North Avenue, a main thoroughfare in their Manhattan neighborhood. Through her comings and goings, with Jonathan in the baby carriage, Carla greeted her neighbors with smiles and hellos. One woman, Bernice Shandelman, who Carla would always see near Sach's fabric shop, took a genuine interest in Jonathan. She and Carla struck up a lasting friendship.

Fast-forward a decade: the Shandelman's son, Bezalel, attended the yeshiva in New Rochelle, where the Schippers had moved. Bernie, coming home from Shabbos services, commented on the quality of a yeshiva boy's layning and thought that the student may have been Bezalel. Carla called his mother to pass on the compliment. Bernice suggested that perhaps her son could give Jonathan Hebrew lessons. Bezalel agreed and this positive relationship of learning and camaraderie had an enormous influence on Jonathan. Their time together paved the path for his bar mitzvah.

Jonathan turned thirteen in January 1970. Carla and Bernie wanted him to have his bar mitzvah on a Rosh Chodesh, the beginning of a new Hebrew month, in this case, the Hebrew month of Adar, which fell on March 13, 1970. A bus was rented in order to accommodate the many friends that were to be a part of the celebration at Anshei Shalom in New Rochelle. Jonathan read from the Torah on that Sunday and several weeks later on Shabbos, he read his haftarah.

> He layned parshas HaHodesh from the Safer Torah. That is the important thing. He gave a speech. This is what he wanted to do. If he was a little bit nervous or a little bit not right, he can't get the words out. But the thoughts are all there in his mind. Jonathan always wants to get it just right.

**

Although Jonathan had made great strides in his development, the Schippers still felt that he desperately needed interaction with others his age.

For three weeks during the summer of 1970, the Schippers vacationed at the Lakehouse Hotel in Woodridge, New York. The hotel offered a day camp, where, unfortunately, Jonathan garnered little interaction. However, while watching him at play by the pool, Carla overheard a conversation about a camp for special-needs children at Camp Ramah in Palmer, Massachusetts, called Tikvah. In early 1971, Carla and Bernie met with Herb Greenberg. This meeting unbolted a sea of forward-thinking ideas, opportunities, and possibilities about Jonathan's potential and the greater needs of all those afflicted with Down syndrome in the 1970s, a time of limited opportunity.

"It was all too common for most professionals and parents to view youngsters with Down syndrome as passive recipients of services," explains Herb Greenberg.

> Educating these children at home and in the community required enormous expenditures of time and patience. Therefore, one was likely to find few, if any, children or young adults with Down syndrome who could select their own clothing, prepare simple meals at home, make their beds each morning, travel on simple errands in the community, and eventually learn to travel on their own. Carla and Bernie remained steadfast in their determination to provide Jonathan with as much autonomy as possible.

Carla and Bernard enrolled Jonathan in the Tikvah program for the summer 1971 season. "For a number of reasons, the Schipper family became a professional inspiration to my wife, Barbara, and me," explains Greenberg.

> Jonathan, fourteen years old, was the first camper with Down syndrome enrolled in our program. As such, he became a curiosity throughout the camp. During our preadmission interview, Carla made it abundantly clear to us that Jonathan's success in our program would be related to the degree of normalization offered to him. At home and in the community, Jonathan's parents would not tolerate any inappropriate behaviors on his part. These behaviors often elicited pandering, patronizing responses from peers and adults. The Schipper's firm and resolute disciplinary actions in

response to Jonathan's behaviors contrasted sharply with the "infantilizing" of this population in the early 1970s in most American educational settings.

Carla recalls that the Tikvah program "was, in no way, welcomed warmly by the *regular campers'* parents. The director, Herb Greenberg, had to fight the other parents to get these children in—a total of eight."

Miraculously, Jonathan went away for summer sleep-away camp. The Ramah experiment was a success. "Many peers from the mainstream of the camp totally disregarded Jonathan's physical stigmata, a prominent feature of individuals with Down syndrome, and pronounced him to be 'just like everyone else,'" recalls Greenberg.

> Jonathan became the 'working model' for all campers with Down syndrome who participated in our program. Our expectations for this population, which exceeded the goals of most programs in the 1970s, were based, in part, upon our experiences with Jonathan. Most youngsters who returned home after a Tikvah summer had a newly acquired 'identity.' They were proud of their Jewish heritage and, in many cases, encouraged their families to increase their participation in Jewish life.

While Jonathan attended summer camp, Bernie and Carla went to Israel to see what was available for him there. "Maybe we would have moved there for Jonathan. But even going to Israel, we did not find what we were looking for."

Once camp was over, Carla and Bernie had a chance to meet again with Herb Greenberg and the other Tikvah parents. "Now, what is important," explains Carla, "is that the director insisted on a three-day post-camp conference to discuss the children's progress while at camp *and* future plans for getting these children where they should be. We came to the conference, and the parents all say the program is fantastic. But then the children come home, and what do we do now?" Greenberg's attentiveness to the special needs of this population in 1971 was not the norm. He was a beacon of light in the Schippers' dealings with Jonathan. Greenberg explained that during the conference, the Schippers asked the hard questions that most families were reluctant to consider: What will be my child's placement and the extent of his independence during his adult years? What will happen to him after I am gone? What are the financial implications of planning for my child's future? What will be his/her quality of life? These practical questions, which Carla and Bernie were determined to find a formula to answer, led them to become leaders in this group of maverick parents and educators.

Laying a Foundation

The Schippers, and the other parents from the Tikvah program at Ramah, formed Shalaym. The purpose of the organization was to gather ideas in order to answer the questions posed at the conference. Also, it would give the campers an opportunity to get together and socialize. Carla was nominated as Shalaym president.

> All right, so we went back home and see what we could do as a group. I naturally go to the head of JTS (Jewish Theological Seminary), a rabbi. And we tell him what we have to do. We had several meetings. After quite a while, nothing got accomplished. I suggested that maybe, for convenience, we could meet at the conservative shul in New Rochelle. It is a logical meeting place where the children could get together. The rabbi heard about this arrangement, and I get a big reprimand that I am not allowed to do that. Well, that finishes the subject.

Shalaym got off to a rough start, but the group was committed to finding an enriching environment for their children. Inspiration would come from very close to home: Carla's eldest daughter Channa. Carla explained that her eldest daughter became involved with the Anthroposophical Society through a chance meeting with Leon Seidenberg, who would later become Channa's husband. Leon was a follower of this society, a movement created by philosopher Rudolf Steiner in the late 1800s. It can be described as a holistic, organic living, learning, teaching, and caretaking approach to life based on Steiner's belief that "thinking can lead to the reality of the spirit in the world,"[50] according to the book *The Philosophy of Freedom*.

Steiner, influenced by the works of Kant and Goethe, wrote—and wrote profusely—that the thinking mind and the spirit can come together as one. Steiner's philosophies led to the Anthroposophical Society movement. Today, it includes institutes that specialize in learning and teaching this philosophy. Steiner's work also led to the establishment of the Waldorf schools, private schools offering an education based on the tenets of Anthroposophy. Channa became a follower of Anthroposophy, a movement that dually and permanently extricated her from her family and faith, and yet gave her family hope of coming closer to an elevated life for Jonathan.

The Anthroposophical Society founded the Camphill communities: self-reliant communities in North America and Europe, composed of special needs residents and Camphill counselors who also lived in these villages and are followers of Anthroposophy.

In these villages, the residents are encouraged to become active participants in all aspects of daily life, from raising farm animals to making candles, weaving, farming and gardening. Residents' creative needed are nourished through music, drama, and a plethora of the arts. Through the principles of Anthroposophy, residents strive for connecting the wholeness of the spirit, physical being and mind.

"Leon told her all about this kind of life. Channa, having a brother with special needs, naturally was interested," says

Carla. Channa visited a Camphill Village for four weeks in 1971. "She had her independence; she always was independent. It was not the norm in those times. But that's the kind of people we are. My father was that way, and so was Channa."

Carla remembers that Channa was very excited about Camphill. The quality of the villagers' life was so remarkable to her that she and Leon invited Carla and Bernie to come to Upstate New York and take a look during the village's ten-year celebration.

The visit had an enormous impact on Bernie and Carla. The only problem was that the lifestyle did not follow their practice of Judaism. "We decided to start our own Camphill. We had a meeting with the Shalaym parents and described what we saw at Camphill. Then, we explained that we wanted to do the same thing but in a Jewish setting." With enthusiasm, Rosh Pina was born. "Our organization, which had roots from Camp Ramah, grew to 150 individuals."

The name for their endeavor was from the prayer "Hallel." The Rosh Pina is the stone that builders despise and cast off. This name and its implication became the cornerstone of their organization. Carla worked on making the community a reality for ten years.

> We worked very hard for this. Along with myself, Paul Rosenfeld, a counselor from Camp Ramah, worked tirelessly. First of all, understand that Bernie and I were strangers in this country. We didn't want to be completely exclusive or offend anyone. We decided that the community would embrace a traditional Jewish experience. But we did not want any particular stamp on this place—Conservative or Orthodox, or Reform. The common factor was that all the people wanted their children in a Jewish environment. The age of the residents would have ranged from fourteen years and up.

Big ideas come with a steep price tag. Eventually, this idea of a Jewish village for special-needs individuals needed money. "I remember going to their apartment and sitting around their dining-room table," recalls Paul Rosenfeld. "We'd do mailings and plan fundraisers and programs for the children and parents. Carla and Bernie had this quiet determination. They were the glue that held the hope of Rosh Pina together. They wanted Jonathan to do things, to have his independence. They knew that he had his limitations. I saw firsthand their frustration and how they dealt with it." Carla and Bernie, with Paul, who was a law student at St. John's University, began solicitations with brochures, literature, and face-to-face meetings. Roadblocks sprang up right away.

> People would say, what about the Federation [Jewish Federation, an umbrella agency overseeing societal, financial and cultural issues and organizations of the Jewish community]? So I go to the Federation and explain what I want to do and talk with the big shots; I ask not for money, but their seal of approval. We needed their blessing to come to other people and organizations to make it legitimate. That is when I came head-to-head with the big shots. Really. We didn't want money, just approval. It was so important to have that in those years. But just ideas—the Federation didn't believe in that.

Herb and Barbara Greenberg of Ramah suggested that the Schippers should speak with one of their camp's big contributors. They thought that the Camphill-inspired idea and the philanthropist might make for a good fit.

> We had meetings. This contributor was willing to give but he wanted everyone else to give too. We spent every Sunday driving and looking for houses. We knew what we wanted: a house and grounds to build on for

later. But we didn't have the money. This was our original problem. So his potential contribution was retracted.

Somehow, Rosh Pina, under Carla's leadership, found a way to finance the purchase of a house near Port Jervis, New York, in 1979. After ten long complicated years, Rosh Pina was close to becoming a reality: a place for the Jewish special needs community to live and qualified volunteers to enrich their vocations. The search for Jonathan's place seemed almost over.

> In order to open a community like this, we had to get a license from the state. In the meantime, there was a rabbi who headed several nursing homes, who defrauded the New York Medicaid system. So the government, more aware, imposed more strict regulations on these types of communities, like Rosh Pina. We had several meetings with the government. I wanted Rosh Pina to have the same low profile as Camphill. This did not sit well with the government. They did not agree with the philosophy of Camphill. Mentioning their leniency with them was a mistake. They were willing to license Rosh Pina as a group home. I refused that because I knew that a group home is a place where you sleep and eat and go to a workshop. Workshops were the worst things. They were nothing but baby-sitting. This was not the purpose of Rosh Pina. I said no. And so it ended after ten years in 1980. I had to give it up.

Her noble efforts to build Rosh Pina, spanning a decade, failed. "After Rosh Pina, we scaled back. But it was like the wind was blown out of us," explains Paul. "We didn't get it, because we had nothing to show for it," says Carla.

Nothing except Jonathan.

Finding His Place

Jonathan's life was dull. Carla would drive him to the Association for Retarded Citizens workshop in White Plains in the morning, and Jonathan would take the bus back at night. Sometimes this led to complications. "He didn't want to do the repetitive nonsense work. Many times, he would fall asleep on the bus and miss his stop. If the bus driver noticed, he would bring him back to his stop eventually."

Jonathan was living at home, withering socially and intellectually. Both Carla and Bernie knew their search was far from done. They continued to look for potential job situations that would give Jonathan an enriching experience. Hits and misses abounded. Herb Greenberg recommended calling up an organization called Ohel, an umbrella agency for Jewish individuals who have emotional and developmental problems. Ohel had established some group homes called Bais Ezra. Herb felt that a Bais Ezra home could be a good environment in which Jonathan could thrive.

In April 1981, Jonathan, twenty-four years old, moved into Bais Ezra, although the loose adherence to an Orthodox lifestyle did not dovetail well at all with the Schippers' strict religious observance. "We were not so young anymore, so we made a trade off." Jonathan stayed at Bais Ezra for three and a half years. At the time, the neighborhood was not content with the group home as a neighbor. "This was in April 1981. Today it is acceptable to have a group home in your neighborhood, but back then, it was not unusual for people to think that there was a danger or something about living near these types of people." Carla and Bernie were still not satisfied with Jonathan's situation. "We were always trying to educate and teach Jonathan more."

In the fall of October 1981, Jedidjah's son, Asher Gross, was bar mitzvahed in Israel. Carla, Bernie and Jonathan attended. During their stay, a gentleman, Mr. Kaniel, approached Bernie and Carla and asked them about Jonathan. He told them that at Hadassah WIZO Institute, Professor Reuven Feuerstein was conducting cognitive studies on individuals just like Jonathan. The family visited the cognitive studies department at the institute and saw promise in Feuerstein's program. They returned to Israel the following year to begin work with their son.

Professor Feuerstein's cognitive enrichment program offered a unique way for Jonathan to become independent and self-sufficient. Carla remembers that the professor immediately recognized Jonathan's intelligence potential.

The Structural Cognitive Modifiability and Mediated Learning Experience and the Feuerstein Method, developed by Feuerstein, capitalize on the strengths in an individual's intelligence. His practice emphasizes the brain's ability to be flexible and accommodating to any situation, regardless of the task, the trauma or gene design.

His teaching methods with Jonathan were extremely successful. Back home in New York with a tutor, Jonathan continued flourishing under the Feuerstein principles.

Professor Feuerstein also felt that facial surgery, which was promoted at the time, would be beneficial. "Coincidentally, we had already read about this in the *Hadassah Magazine* and discussed the matter with Jonathan."

In 1984, the Schippers met with surgeon, Dr. Peled, in Ein Kerem Hadassah Hospital to discuss the facial surgery. "He said that he would take away the fat underneath his chin and put prostheses into his cheeks. He explained that he would not touch Jonathan's eyes because of possible scarring. He said that he would alter his mouth and tongue so Jonathan could swallow and eat easier. But he also said that it was likely that the tongue's thickness would grow back."

The surgery to alleviate Jonathan's appearance was not his first. Unfortunately, many medical problems can accompany a Down-syndrome child, including epilepsy, heart defects, premature aging, cataracts, thyroid problems, and skeletal abnormalities.[51]

Jonathan's first bout with surgery occurred in 1969, during Passover. Jonathan was taken to the hospital because of a major loss of blood in his stool. He was diagnosed with Meckel's Diverticulum, bleeding in the intestinal tract. "This happens a lot with Down-syndrome individuals," says Carla. "We had a problem finding a surgeon because in those years, doctors didn't want to operate on Down-syndrome individuals. For what reason, I don't know. Maybe the fear that we would do something if it went wrong." Finally, a friend of Carla's, a Dutch anesthesiologist, found Dr. Paul Poppers, a surgeon at Columbia Presbyterian Hospital, who was willing to perform the surgery. "Imagine, at twelve, having a major surgery. He recuperated very nicely."

Jonathan battled pneumonia after his facial surgery at Hadassah Hospital. Carla and Bernie rented an apartment nearby and stayed with him every day until he fully recovered. "Jonathan took it like a giant."

> We had rented an apartment in Rachel Emuna, but I was sitting with him day and night for five days because he could not be left alone in the hospital. It was a small room with bookcases, a bed, and a chair. That's it. You cannot leave a person like that in the

hospital. The kid, twenty-six years old, took it all in stride. Once Jonathan recuperated, we returned to the States; but after several months, there was a slight complication. We noticed that one cheek was slightly red, different from the other one. Immediately we called Dr. Peled. He told us that the prosthesis had to come out because he felt it was not right. However, this procedure could be done in the States. Dr. Peled recommended a colleague who performed the procedure. So we did it in New York. After the doctor removed the prosthesis, Jonathan asked the doctor if he could keep it. The doctor asked him what he would do with it and he didn't give it to him.

In 1985, the Schippers returned to Israel to see Dr. Peled. He asked for the prosthesis.

"We didn't have it because the doctor in the States refused Jonathan's request. Can you believe that? Jonathan had to repeat the procedure again. He never complained." Unfortunately, a few years later that same prosthesis had to be removed yet again. This time, a dental assistant performed that procedure "under horrible circumstances. It was terrible. She wasn't used to doing it. I was furious. But he took it all in stride."

The unsuccessful surgeries and lack of stimulation began to take its toll. Jonathan continued living at Bais Ezra, but slowly things began to crumble. Jonathan's medication stopped being administered correctly. He grew bored. He was not mentally stimulated. His only responsibility was to attend a workshop geared toward the cerebral-palsy residents. He gained too much weight. He rebelled. He ate from garbage cans on the way home from the workshop. It was not a good fit. The mindless tasks were dead ends. Carla and Bernie decided that it was not working.

In 1988, Jonathan moved back home to Pelham Road in New Rochelle. His only form of stimulation was to go back to the Association for Retarded Citizens (ARC) in White Plains. He also volunteered with Carla, doing clerical tasks at the Southeast Consortium that housed an after-school program. Meanwhile, Carla kept in touch with the Shalaym/ Rosh Pina parents.

In 1988, parents from this effort who were living in Fort Worth, Texas, told Carla and Bernie that they were opening up a private home in Coral Springs, Florida.

> We went to Coral Springs and met with the people. It was five young men. Each resident would have his or her own room and a Jewish couple as the parents. We discussed the pros and cons of Jonathan living in Florida in this type of setting. In the end, we agreed to it. It was very expensive, twenty-five thousand dollars a year. As I look back, I cannot imagine that we did these things. Unbelievable. It seemed that overall it was working out. However, eventually we saw that the couple that was in charge was not the right people. It turned out that they didn't know how to do the bookkeeping. The man had Tourette's syndrome. The woman had a part-time job, so she couldn't give her full attention to the residents. They were fired, but then they hired someone who didn't know kashruth. So in December 1989, we had to take him out.

Jonathan was back in New Rochelle. Carla was seventy-two years old. Bernie was seventy. By 1993, Herb Greenberg insisted that Carla and Bernie give Bais Ezra a second try. Ohel was opening a new home in the Flatbush section of Brooklyn. "I was never too happy to send him to Brooklyn. Eventually, he started wearing a *black hat* [representing a certain very religious lifestyle]. We didn't have much of a choice, though. The good thing about it was they knew him."

This is where Jonathan lives today. Carla and Bernie are satisfied with this second Bais Ezra experience. When Jonathan first moved in, he performed workshop responsibilities but he progressed quickly to the rehabilitation area for higher performing adults. Jonathan works on the computer and types in the weekly newsletter. He enjoys the clerical tasks of stuffing envelopes, collating paper, and other office responsibilities. He attends the HASC (Hebrew Academy for Special Children) Center for day habilitation. Carla says that he is well liked. About three years ago, Bais Ezra began a theatrical performance program. Jonathan thrives as a cast member, most recently as the lead, Willy Wonka.

"He is very satisfied. He always wanted to have a job and move out. That was his goal, to become independent."

Holland

Carla's parents, Joseph and Johanna Nathans

The TECALEI Club, Leida van Tyn,
Carla Nathans and Tetta Hazekamp

Close friend Emil Mendelson and Carla

Wedding Day, Carla and Andre Andriesse,
August 26, 1938

ON WOODEN WHEELS 185

Andre and Channa in Enschede

Andre's identification card.
He was picked up one week after this card was issued.

Last photograph of Andre, taken before he was
picked up on September 14, 1941.

Jedidjah, while hiding, in Marle.
Carla does not know who took this photograph.

Channa, while hiding, in Veenendaal, under the care of the Thoomes family. This photograph, as well as a few others, were taken by Ellie Thoomes, and smuggled to Carla while she was hiding in Marle.

Carla's forged identification card

The Schipper brothers, Henry and Bernie,
on the Koop farm after the war.

Juut and Philip de Groot

Jedidjah, Bernie, Ruthie, Carla, and Channa in
Marle, visiting the Mulders after the war.

The girls, Channa, Ruthie, and Jedidjah

Jedidjah and Channa on Wadsworth Avenue
in New York.

Jonathan's bar mitzvah

TECALEI Club in Switzerland

Channa and Carla in New Rochelle, New York

Andreas and Julian Seidenberg

Bernard Schipper

From generation to generation: Children, grandchildren and great-grandchildren. Michah and Jedidjah Gross, *third and fourth from left*, and Ruthie and Yaakov Goldstein, *six and seventh from left*. At the wedding of Gedalyahu Goldstein and Tzippora Wise, June 2004, Israel.

Carla, Jonathan, and Bernie in Jacksonville, Florida

Jonathan as Willy Wonka

Filtered by Heart and Mind: Voices of the Daughters

Channa Andriesse Seidenberg

In the fall of 2004, I had the opportunity to speak on the phone with Carla's eldest daughter, Channa. Our conversations took place on two consecutive Sunday mornings. Channa lives in Upstate New York and was preparing to go to Basel, Switzerland, for a six-week internship at the Anthroposophical Society's headquarters.

Our conversations were very relaxed and comfortable. Her voice shares her mother's light girlish lilt. Channa's husband, Leon, at the time of the interviews, was suffering from advanced stages of diabetes. Channa was struggling with his increasingly demanding care-giving needs at their home. After our conversations, his health rapidly declined. In February 2005, he passed away.

Q: Why do you use "Andriesse" in your name?

A: I inserted the maiden name five or six years ago. I feel more whole when I have the full name. I can't even really answer why.

Q: What are some of your childhood memories?

A: My first own real memory is of a walk down a residential street in Holland with wonderful trees and sunlight in front of houses. I guess I was with my mother. The baby [Jedidjah] was already there because I remember that there was a baby carriage. There was piano music coming from a window. It was—I know *now* that it was—"Peer Gynt Suite" by [Edvard] Grieg. It was such a striking experience for me. I was conscious of myself and what was outside. I must have been almost three. She, the baby, was very tiny. It must have been May or June. It was so striking. That was the whole beginning of my awareness.

There was a lot of singing in my home. My father was a cantor. I must have heard a lot of music in the synagogue and at home. I have a feeling that my mother's grandmother was a singer. I never understood that, because they were Orthodox Jews; but I know that someone said she was an opera singer. I have no idea about my father's side. I know very little about his heritage. I think she [the grandmother] died during the war. In my later childhood there was a lot of music. I am sure there was a piano as well.

Q: Do you remember your house in Enschede?

A: I am not aware of any physical surroundings. I knew what the house and larger surroundings looked like. I met the house after the war, but I didn't recognize anything.

Q: What do you remember before the war?

A: I have to say that one cannot actually analyze a child experience. I come from a very spiritual foundation. I am not a practicing Jew. I haven't practiced since I was twenty-one.

Q: Could you explain that in more detail?

A: It is the idea that the human being is developing in stages. I had this experience of self and world; a child sees himself as separate. My answers will reflect that philosophy. I remember very little from before the war. In hindsight, I could identify the atmosphere around me. There was always a threat. We always had to quickly move across the street. Everything was fearful. I remember it was very dark. The sunlight was very striking. But everything was very dark.

Q: Tell me what you remember about your father, Andre.

A: What you should know is that I had a very special relationship with this human being, more so than with my mother. I know this in my bones. I remember playing with him. It was very clear that he and I had a lot to do with each other. That is usually based on my knowledge of the situation of previous incarnation. I know the amazing worth that radiated between us.

Q: Do you remember when he was taken?

A: I knew he wasn't there immediately. My mother relates that I constantly asked about him. It must have driven her crazy. This has played a huge role in my life—this not being able to grieve because I didn't know what happened.

Q: Do you remember going into hiding?

A: This going away is not a memory at all. I came alone. The only thing I remember is that when I arrived at my foster parents' house I was carried in. I remember somehow that incident and being received very lovingly.

Q: Tell me about your foster parents.

A: A very wonderful couple, Jan and Ellie Thoomes. He was a reverend of a Protestant church and head of a school right next to the house, and it still is there. It was in Veenendaal, in the middle of the country.

Jan was a very spiritual man. One day after lunch, I overheard him saying, "Mother, I am going upstairs to meditate." When I became older, I became aware later of that. Maybe I am just reading into the statement. There was a lot going on with kids running around and maybe he just wanted time alone, but this stayed with me.

Q: What are your memories from hiding?

A: I have inklings and pictures of things, not memories but vignettes. It was a wonderfully ordered and structured home. There was a piano. That was very important. In hindsight, it was a bit strict. They did have a serving girl, but it was not an aristocratic home.

In the war I had to call them "mama" and "papa." That was because of the danger of having a child there that was not the family's child. They had contact with the Resistance. I was a dark-haired child. The foster father was dark haired, the mother was blond. Across the road, there were dark children. I have a feeling that children were told not to talk about this. I remember playing with these kids later on in the war. I wasn't the only one they hid. There were two brothers that came also from Rotterdam. I used to know their names. I have the names somewhere in a photographic album that Tante Ellie made. She was an amateur photographer. The album was a gift from her. When we left, she handed each of us an album with pictures. This has been such a tremendous gift.

I don't remember if calling her "mama" confused me.

I remember "Sinter Klaas." Obviously, this is a Christian legend. It may be a real spiritual being who was Spanish. Sinter Klaas did lots and lots of good works. He was from a rich family and helped the poor and did it surreptitiously, leaving money during the night. He traveled from Spain to the Netherlands. He had a servant who was a black man, a Moor, who committed a sin and had his tongue cut out. He carried all the packages. On December 5 in Amsterdam, in the afternoon, I remember the scene of the saint arriving in town, coming on a huge horse. People would line the street, and he would travel down the street, walking very slowly with the horse next to him. That evening, there would be this wonderful celebration of games and poems and good things to eat. Things were always served that night. Children were told that in the middle of the night he would travel on roofs with his horse and leave mandarins, gifts, chocolate, and peanuts. That was very special. The birthday was on December 6, which is my wedding day, a day of celebration and gifts. This was also celebrated in Jewish homes because it was ingrained in the Dutch folklore. I celebrated this with my foster parents. Advent was celebrated also. I had a cardboard house with red cellophane in the windows. It was beautiful. I can still see the light reflected in the red cellophane. And there was a Christmas tree and singing.

This was the culture in the home.

The memories of the negative aspects are stronger near the end of the war during the *Hongerwinter* in 1944. Everybody was starving. I remember strongly, we would also go foraging for berries in the summertime.

The only time I remember being unhappy is when I was being washed. I remember a picture of the sink and not being happy.

I remember wearing glasses. I had a weak eye, and they couldn't correct the weak eye.

Because there was no food, the foster parents had to give me over to their servants. I went to one of their parents, who were farmers. I remember being afraid of one of the servant girls. I just remember this feeling of fear.

Q: Do you remember the Nazi presence in Veenendaal?

A: I remember the time the Germans entered the town in a tank. I was playing in the attic at a friend's house with a wooden hobbyhorse. We were called down. We had to stand in the entryway with our backs against the wall. The soldiers came in and took out all the toys, and we never saw them again. I have no idea why they did this. We had fear from the adults.

Q: What about the Liberation?

A: I remember the Canadians coming in tanks. We lined the streets and they threw down candy, chocolates, and peppermints, and it was like heaven. I remember it so strongly because I had a roll of peppermints that I didn't open. And I carried it with me, which leads me to my mother picking me up [from my foster parents].

Q: Do you recall being reunited with your mother?

A: After the war, when she came to pick me up. She was at the front door. There was a long hall, and I ran to her. It was very striking. We went home in a truck with other people. We arrived at this pension that we were going to stay in for a while in Enschede. It was a house that belonged to two ladies who came back [from the war] and opened it up to us. I met my sister for the first time. I was a little threatened. She was cute as a button. I came back from the war very malnourished, with a distended body and dysentery.

In Enschede, we put some order back in our lives. I had to put my peppermints in a safe place. I remember that after a nap they were eaten into. This was a tremendous threat to me.

My mother, of course, met my stepfather, Bernard. She made a real connection to him. I think that is what got my mother together. They got married in 1946. We moved away from the pension and moved into our own home. Those years were extremely difficult for me. I became more introverted, although I was a child that loved to laugh. I had a good sense of humor. I am sure that had to do with the whole childhood experience.

Q: Why were you so introverted?

A: Nothing overtly happened, but I was very, very resentful of my second father. He is a dear man. I felt he usurped a position that I could not allocate to him. I don't think he had that problem with my sister. That feeling continued until I could consciously analyze it.

Also, I was cross-eyed. So I always had people looking at me. My parents decided to do something about it. I was operated on for "readjustment," but they adjusted too far. I was seven at the time.

School was not a positive experience. In 1950, I was ten or something. I went to a Jewish school in Amsterdam. That was more horrendous than public school. So was one of the teachers. That was the "wall eyed" period. Until I was twelve, I was hounded and pestered, and other children and adults would stare at me. So I became more and more introverted in a way. Our clothes were less than what everyone had. Our shoes were imported from a kind aunt in America that was not the fashion. I actually was a left-handed child, converted to right hand. Today, I still write with my right hand.

During all those years after the war, I was ill a lot. I was taken to many tests. I had to do the second grade over again because I was having so many medical tests. I remember that my mother took me to the south of Holland, a Catholic region. We were in the waiting room, I saw on the wall a figure with a cross. I said, "Mom, what is that man doing hanging there?" She went white. That was my first experience of a crucifixion.

Aside from the eye, it was always interpreted that something was wrong with my thyroid. It wasn't so. But I wasn't getting better. The tests were complicated and not very pleasant. They used a graph. There would be a machine. A needle. You had to lie still for a long time.

Those were the years. It is very interesting. I also had scarlet fever when I was eight or so. I was treated at home. People had to come in white garb and everything was very aseptic.

At twelve, I had another eye operation, which did correct some of it. The emotional trauma of being teased brought my parents to the school, but they couldn't do much about it because it was already near the end of the school year. The question was: would I go to the Jewish school or someplace else?

They took me to a psychologist... poor man. He administered Rorschach tests, the whole deal. The psychologist asked me about my father. I wouldn't say one word. After a time, he concluded that I was of less than average intelligence. It was a good thing he did. Instead of sending me to another horrendous Jewish school, I was sent to the lowest level, HBS. They chose to send me to Ulo, a Montessori school. That was the best thing that ever happened to me. There was music, arts, nature, and crafts, and I had my first girlfriend. One was free to select your courses.

I was free. I was able to breathe. It was a loving environment. It was the best thing that ever happened to me. In Amsterdam, I always wanted to study voice, but my parents couldn't afford the lessons. At nine, I studied piano. I had lessons with someone in the conservatory. I remember the double door and I could listen to the student practice that came before me.

Q: What went through your mind while you were hiding?

A: It is hard to go back to this stage. Let me say this. I certainly had questions when I was younger. When I was in hiding, I hadn't evolved to where I could think about things. Things happened back then, I didn't think of as good or bad, they just were. It is what it is. It just happened to be. Only later, in my twenties, could I think or question. I often had to think, what did a human being have to go through to create these awful things? Not, these awful things happened. There was no life threat. The adults who were hiding me, for them, yes. I wasn't aware. I wasn't put in a concentration camp. As a child, it just was how it was. In the case of being with my foster parents, I couldn't reflect, oh, how awful, I lost my mom and dad. There I was, going through these experiences. Only later on come the questions and the illnesses. It has affected me.

When I was in my twenties, I thought, "How is it possible that human beings can treat each other this way?"

Q: When did you find out about the Holocaust, the concentration camps, and the results of the war?

A: Not until the preteens did I learn about what went on during the war. This whole waking up of the thinking possibilities happens around nine years old. I knew that there was very little family left. We heard about the Anne Frank thing. I had more awareness but no judgment yet. Only questions. I wasn't interested in the present time. I was an avid reader, reading books about medieval happenings, the Renaissance... pre-medieval.

Q: Did you discuss the Holocaust with your parents?

A: I must have somewhere felt that this was something that one didn't talk about. It would be painful for my mother to talk about. I never addressed it. I wasn't a very proactive child anyway. I never have talked to Bernie about what happened. A turning point for both my mother and me came in 1990 or 1991. I went to a psychiatrist in New York. Her name was Ada Nicolcu, a Romanian woman who was ten years my senior. She spent the war in Romania. My doctor sent me to her. I asked my mother if she had pictures of my father and she gave me the photographs. We had a wonderful conversation. From then on, I had much more compassion for her whole situation. This compassion woke up in me. The whole marriage/remarriage . . .

Q: Did you talk about the war with Jedidjah or Ruthie?

A: I have never talked about the experiences about the war with Jedidjah. She did initiate a search at Mauthausen. She found that our father wasn't on the list of the memorial. I found out later that lots of others' names weren't there either. An additional monument with the names was added. She researched that. We talked about that. And then I also was sent from her a book about Mauthausen. I don't have deep conversations with Ruthie either. We talk always about practical things. Nothing deep. More about the present situation. I don't think Jonathan knows about that time.

Q: What happened with the Thoomes family? Did you keep in touch?

A: I visited the Thoomes once a year after the war ended. They had four boys all in all. It was very different. The two boys that they also hid, one has passed away and the other died in an accident. Both Thoomeses have passed on. In the beginning of 1984, I went to Holland to be present at a celebration of people that had hidden with the people still alive. I was the one still alive. They were given a medal of honor [through Yad Vashem's Righteous Among the Nations in Jerusalem]. That was very important to them. Extremely important. This was done in Den Haag [The Hague], Holland. All their children were there as well.

Q: Do you have any contact with other children that were hidden?

A: I don't know of any others that were hidden. I have very little contact with anyone there. So few are left.

Q: Tell me about living in the United States.

I was only at Ulo for two years when my parents said that we were moving to America. I said that I don't want to go. But you go. I had been transported to two places. My whole security was taken away. I had to go. That was another horrendous experience. My half sister was born in 1947 [Ruthie], so there we went.

My father had a job right away as a mechanic. My mother was an excellent, excellent dressmaker. She started working from home and joined a woman who did work downtown. We lived in an apartment in Washington Heights. I really had to take responsibilities. My mother would leave a menu, and I would have to follow through.

School life was horrendous. I didn't speak English, so I had to go back to the eighth grade. I had a very hard time. The kids called me Hannah. I told them that that's not my name. It was Channa. But they called me Hannah banana—children are terribly cruel.

When I was eleven, I went to summer camp. They were religious Jewish camps. During one of those summers, I experienced something very strong. In a study group, we discussed free will. That made such an impact on me. Do we have free will? I lived with that for three years. That led to a different spiritual path for my life. I graduated eighth grade and I went to George Washington High School. There, I had more freedom, and I could choose my courses. I took Hebrew and Latin. I had a wonderful old lady for a Latin teacher. In high school, I started composing and improvising on the piano. It was primitive. I didn't know theory. I played it for a neighbor who pooh-poohed it. But it didn't have impact on me. I joined B'nai Akivah, and I started a choral group. It was just marvelous. I had a great experience. Those were my high school years. It was very good.

My physical body with puberty became a lumpy figure, and I always had a problem with weight. I didn't want to go directly to college. I wanted to earn money to go back to Holland to see what I left behind. A year later, I went back.

I found a job in a Jewish administrative office. I lived in a Jewish home for students. I was friendly with a family from a different town. They were wonderful. The woman was in her early thirties. Her husband was the cantor or rabbi. They had a deaf, blind son. I was very close with her. I may have talked to her about my experience [of hiding]. I could imagine that because we were so close. It was an absolutely wonderful time. I was still Orthodox. I remember a lot of laughter. I was able to take part in the cultural life. I became familiar with the literature. I had interesting experiences in the Jewish community and being in the States.

But the thinking in this community was very narrow. There were certain ideas that I couldn't accept. So I went back home. I began asking questions. I wasn't comfortable with all the laws coming from the outside. Six hundred and thirteen laws is a restricting life, unless you can rise above the idea of being in a cage. Many Orthodox can do this because they are spiritually connected, and that is being a good Jew.

Q: Where did this path lead?

A: I went back to New York and lived in a room in a neighborhood house. This was my first taste of freedom. I got a job and went back to school at Hunter College. I met an Israeli girl at school and shared an apartment with her. That was the beginning of leaving Judaism. I had a very simplistic view of the power and wrath of God. I needed more spirituality.

I met a girl in the early 1960s and all the civil rights marches, and I was pulled into that. She had a lot of friends. This was the first time in my life that I had Chinese food or a hamburger.

I started voice studies in 1963 with a private teacher. That was the turning point. I joined a big chorus and semiprofessional chorus. I studied German. I was very interested in musical German literature. By that time, I was wondering why Americans were against all German products. I couldn't understand it. I couldn't make the connection between how the outer product, a Volkswagen, would be connected to German history. I still feel that is the wrong connection. Sometimes when I meet someone in Germany of a certain age, I always question, "Where were you?" I have colleagues who were youths, and I know of other persons who were in the Hitler Youth group. But we didn't talk. We know our biographies. They were children then and that leads back to human development.

I was looking for a spiritual direction. By this time, I had moved to Riverside Drive and Ninety-Seventh Street with a young woman, and we were both working. I met my husband then. He lived on the fifth floor, and I on the fourth. He had a Dachshund, Opa.

I was coming home at night around ten or eleven, from rehearsal. I had all this music in my arms. He and I went up in the elevator. He said he studied voice for six years. He and the dog came to my house. We had a cup of coffee and stayed up until three in the morning. He told me all about Anthroposophy.

Jonathan was born in 1957. I knew he was what we called Mongoloid, but I knew he was developmentally bright. I couldn't mention this to my parents. He was the only male in an Orthodox family, the spiritual heir in the family. The males are more important. This was very painful for them and this could not be mentioned. I admire what they did for him . . . really, to get him to be as normal as possible.

When I met Leon, he brought me literature about Rudolf Steiner. One of the things he developed was work with Mongoloid children. The identification was more negative than anything else. I read that their skin is very sensitive and they always should wear warm woolly clothes to keep them comfortable, in their warmth.

After a few weeks, I called my parents and told them about this. I got such a strong reaction. My mother began to cry. My father got on the phone and started yelling at me. He said that that word was never to be used and hung up on me. I didn't talk to them for a very long time.

I went to Camphill, a worldwide movement for the developmentally disabled. It helps them for life. You are taken care of. Food, clothing, expenses. It is a life choice. I was interested in doing a practicum there in relationship to my brother. It was an overwhelming joy when I got there. Lots of crafts, gardening, farming, weavery, candle making, woodworking shop, horses, pigs, and cows. I spent the summer there and had a wonderful time and learned so much about the disabled adults. I wanted my parents to see this. I invited them and they came.

Q: What did they think of Camphill?

A: They came there, were impressed and that began Rosh Pina. They wanted a Camphill with a Jewish spiritual element. Karl Conig, who was Jewish and had an amazing experience of Christianity, started this Camphill. The first one was in Scotland. I was not involved with Rosh Pina. I was engaged in my own sort of journey.

Q: Explain.

A: I was handed a lyre. It has to do with my further path in music. I learned to play it. I was invited to the first conference of lyre players. I stayed in New York for a year. I then went to Europe in 1975. My fiancé, Leon, had already gone to Switzerland to study artistic eurhythmy: visible speech and tone. He was in his mid-forties and a diabetic. He went near Basel, and I went near Bern. We came back in 1980 from Switzerland. He spoke the German language brokenly. It was frustrating. He had a hard time with the language.

Q: You and Leon have two sons. Tell me about them.

A: Maybe December 6, 1975, I had a miscarriage. Then Andre our son was born June 1977. I was already an old parent. I didn't have such an easy time giving birth. We went to Camphill Village in the States. We lived there for five years. I began an orchestra of hand bells and other instruments. I have been doing that since 1981. We had our first benefit in 1986 at Alice Tully Hall. We were the last offering. We had a few minutes of music and ten minutes of standing ovation and crying.

It has become a bitter experience because it has become political. I am not fond of these huge concerts anymore.

My son, Andre Michalis, is twenty-seven, born in June 1977. He is in Germany, near Lake Constance. He is trained in social therapy, working with Down syndrome and young adults and adults developmentally disabled. He is also interested in biodynamic farming. Presently, he is working in a factory where they produce cleaning products that are environmentally sound. It is a small place. Andre has Jedidjah's energy. Wonderful, gifted guy. Difficult.

Julian Elmo David Andriesse Seidenberg, twenty-four, is in Olympia, Washington. He's the one I can have conversations with. He's my soul buddy. He was born in March 1980. He is just finding himself. He was not academically gifted. Julian had borderline ADD [Attention Deficit Disorder] and is amazing with his hands. He learned through doing with his hands. He's learned leatherwork with a master and now is building houses. He is a musician. A drummer. He and I are amazing. We improvise together. He doesn't understand what is going on here, with Leon. He doesn't have the patience.

Q: Have you shared your experience during World War II with your family?

A: They know of my history. They don't know much. I long to bring them to Enschede. This linking is important. Leon is aware. He himself has had a traumatic childhood.

Q: I understand that you had a bout with cancer.

A: I was a housemother and Leon a housefather at Camphill in Upstate New York. We had eight villagers. My husband was the head of the enamel workshop.

I got cancer there. In April 1988, they discovered colon cancer. I had surgery in Hudson. I had therapy in

Arlesheim, Switzerland. I did not choose chemotherapy. Emotionally, the therapy was very important for me. My husband watched everything I ate. He said that I have to stay alive for my kids. And I said that I have to keep alive for me. I joined a cancer group based on the work of Dr. Bernie Siegel, and I became aware of the mind/body connection

Q: Explain your therapy.

A: Lawrence LeShan, an amazing psychotherapist with twenty-five years of research with terminally ill patients said that you can fight for your life. The majority of those with traumatic illness had traumatic childhood experiences . . . a parent would leave or divorce or death, maybe a loss of a brother or sister. What happens to the child? The child takes on the guilt of whatever has happened in its life. This is the feeling of rejection. This happens very early on. What happens is that the person thinks that he has to prove that he or she is good enough. And this proving happens on and on throughout their life. This "Please say that I am good enough." This happens on the outside, but there is no acknowledgment on the inside. This ongoing process of negating can lead to the cancer. That realization needs to be worked on. You need to see the child again. One learns to look at the child with compassion. You finally work on the realization as an adult that the child is not responsible and there is no guilt. If one is lucky, you come to the point of not blaming the self. This improves the quality of life at the end. The agony of guilt is taken away at the end. This is such an important lesson. If there is an imbalance in a child, it is not because of them. Steiner said that a difficult child in the classroom is not difficult. The teacher needs to see what is blocking the relationship

Q: What was your guilt?

A: My guilt was that my father disappeared. Why did he go? I wasn't good enough? Why did she give me up? I wasn't good enough? I wasn't good enough to keep?

Q: Are you still with Camphill?

A: We decided to move away from Camphill altogether. So we had been away from the world so much that it was hard to reintegrate. My husband got a job in a home, and we rented a small house. Yeah, those were hard times... cancer support groups. I taught adults and children to play the lyre and sing. Musical therapy. That has been what I am doing ever since. Also, I am training for singing therapy. I just finished that this summer. I started three and a half years ago, doing this music therapy. It has been difficult. I hope to develop this work. I would love to join with art therapists and build up a therapeutic center.

It is a very difficult part of my life that is a mirror of my early life. Leon is just seventy-two. He is diabetic. Surprisingly, the doctors say he is doing well. The physical impact is bad. His emotional state is devastating. He retired. That was devastating. I am working with a situation of decline. I don't want to be a caretaker. I still have things to do.

Q: How do you deal with these challenges?

A: If I have a decision to make, or problem, I will turn to a higher world and ask questions. Not so much prayer—which I also do—more offering up, a solution from another realm rather than going around and making myself ill. Laying it aside. Letting go of resistance. Not resisting what needs to come.

Q: Did you find the Anthroposophical Society, or did it find you?

A: If I hadn't been ready for this "learning" of Anthroposophy or sort of a metaphysical observation of human life, I probably would have not been attracted to it.

**

Jedidjah Gross

Carla's home was hot when I arrived at five o'clock for my interview. It was already dark outside as the wind whipped around The Coves. The first of many hurricanes was beginning to make its presence known as I shook hands with Jedidjah Gross. Carla's home was always a little bit warm, and I liked it that way. But today, the heat was not my cozy buddy. It condensed the tense emotions that I felt radiating from everyone in the room. Jedidjah was like a tiger pacing in an unknown cage, namely, her parents' home. She was not happy to see me, or maybe it was just my laptop.

Jedidjah Gross, an Orthodox Jew, lives in the West Bank. Carla tempers this fact with the caveat that in Jedidjah's presence, it is more appropriate to use the biblical term, Shomron. *Jedidjah has five children and thirteen grandchildren. Before coming to Jacksonville, Jedidjah flew first to Holland, staying there for a rabbinical conference in which she was a translator for a friend also in attendance. From there, she flew to New York to visit Ruthie and Jonathan. It was during this visit that Carla unexpectedly fell at Ruthie's. Jedidjah came to Jacksonville to help Carla settle back into her routine. The bottom line: she's a good daughter to make the trip, but she's carrying a lot of emotional baggage along with her. Her visit is only for a few short days.*

"*I thought this was a social visit,*" *Jedidjah bluntly tells me through a forced smile as we sit down at the dining room table. I open my laptop. She crosses her arms.*

I did not come out in torrential winds and rain to have a social visit.

"I didn't realize," *acknowledging her complaint.* "You don't have to answer anything that makes you feel uncomfortable. I'll only go as far as you let me."

I came for an interview and I was going to get one. This exchange will be positively fruitful or pleasantly brief.

Q: Do you have any specific memories of hiding?

A: No.

Alright-y. I can think of more than one way to make a cake. I do not want to offend this woman. She is beautiful. Dark-skinned. Elegant. Yet she has that Israeli edge, that toughness of living on the brink. I completely respect her defensive attitude.

Q: Do you remember your childhood after the war?

A: We had a hard time when we were living there. My mother wasn't well, and I wasn't happy being with her because I had been with people that were loving and affectionate and she wasn't. I lived with an elderly couple that doted on me like an only child. I was hiding in Marle, slightly northwest of Enschede. I was raised *goyish*. They called me "Didikah."

Q: What were your memories of Jan and Pauline Mulder?

A: I went back in 1970 to visit the family. I must have written them a letter to let them know I was coming. They were still alive. She had just had a brain aneurysm. She was blind by that time. Jan took me to the hospital. I think he

was upset that I came because she was so bad. I went to see her. She heard me. And she wanted me to hug her. It is very difficult for me to meet an estranged person in a hospital. They never had any children of their own.
I didn't know that I was hidden behind a cupboard [when the Nazis were in the village]. I don't remember the bedroom. I had a vague sensation of the house, the smells, and keeping an eye on my kids. I brought Tanya who was four and Ashi went, too. He was two.

Q: What else did you choose to do in Holland on that visit?

A: I went there for the purpose of seeing them [the Mulders]. And then I went back to Amsterdam. And then I flew back again to Israel. I think that I stayed overnight.

Q: Do your children remember going?

A: The kids don't remember anything. I've asked them.

Q: Do you remember your feelings as a child after leaving the Mulders?

A: I felt uprooted. I don't remember meeting my sister. I just remember not being a happy camper as the saying goes. Other children that have been hidden feel similar. When there is no bonding from an early age, it is just rough going and it remains that way.

Q: What became of Jan and Pauline?

A: The Mulders have passed. I went back to the house three years ago with my husband and no one is living there. The house was a typical Dutch house. Very steep staircases, very unpleasant staircases. Maybe they were built that way to save space? I remember tiled roofs, or perhaps thatched. The house was on the same property of the school. The school is still there and being used. It just looks more modern.

I talked with someone who was a policeman during the war. He said he came to the house every day during the war and didn't know I was there until after the war. He was a friend of the Mulders. According to my mother, this same policeman plays a big role in her life as well. She may know the name... Jan knew many languages and this policeman went there every day because he could translate things that no one else could.

I was so anxious to talk to anyone that I knew had memories of the war. I saw a person in a window of a house in Marle, and I made my husband stop the car. And I asked her about the war. She invited me in because the woman's father was a policeman, and for the next hour we discussed the war. She had a very heavy Dutch dialect that was hard to understand.

Q: Did you know that in the Mulder house that your mother was being hidden along with another woman, Mrs. Wijnberg?

A: No.

Q: What do you remember about your childhood in Holland after the war?

A: I had very long hair, and my mother braided it. The kids always dipped my hair in the inkwells. My mother got mad at me. She used to say, "How dare you. You got your hair dirty."

I was not a good student at all. I had ADD. I couldn't concentrate. I suppose I had too much going on in my life prior to first grade. I know the symptoms of ADD, and I am quite positive of that. I used to go back to the

Mulders for a week during summer vacation up until we moved. Why? I don't know. I never had the *venue* to ask these questions. [When visiting the Mulders] I somehow felt very different. I knew I was Jewish. They wanted me to go to church with them. I didn't want to, but I did out of respect. I guess because I was a rebel, I would go. But I knew that I was going to be different. I remember that I had a very good friend, Bepie Hooneburg. I liked Holland.

Q: Describe your experience in the United States.

A: The minute we moved here, our past was basically erased. It wasn't referred to often. It was as if it didn't exist. It was always lurking but never confronted. I just didn't want to be in the United States. That may have been a resentment I had because no one addressed the issue. I left friends in Amsterdam, and I knew how difficult that was. That's why we decided to move from Chicago to Israel by the time Tanya [Jedidjah's eldest child] was in the first grade. Moving, it is a major upheaval in someone's life.

Q: You describe yourself as a rebel, yet your parents are Orthodox, and you also feel a strong connection to Judaism. Explain.

A: I was very determined to live in Israel. From the time we came to the United States, I couldn't stand it. I was not quite twelve yet.

Q: In high school, did you ever talk about your war experience with your friends?

A: I went to George Washington High School. In my high school years, World War II never came up. We just didn't talk about that. I had a few friends. I remember one Estonian girl, but I don't remember her name. We went to B'nai Akivah [Orthodox social young-adult group] together. I met Michah through B'nai Akivah.

Q: What are your thoughts on how you handled your Holocaust experience?

A: My past was a non-issue. Because of this, I wasn't so easy to be with. I guess I had a lot of anger. I was angry at my parents. My husband took the brunt of it after we were married. After we moved to Israel, I got help. I was able to confront what I really had gone through. This included the Mulders. And that's why he [Michah] came with me [back to Marle]. *Amcha* [Hebrew, meaning grassroots] is the organization that takes care of people that have gone through the Shoah.

Q: How do you address your past with your children?

A: In Israel, it is much more common to hear about the Shoah. They know about the history. I try to make it not miserable for them. Their life, thank God, is different. They all empathize a different way. We have an open-door policy. I won't start talking out of the blue—but nothing is unapproachable.

Q: Describe your relationship with your sisters Channa and Ruthie.

A: I can't remember being very close. We must have been because we were sisters. I think because of Channa's experiences, she was a lot more mature than I was. She tended to see life through more of an adult vision. She identified with things my mother would say more than I could. It wasn't until after Ruthie got married that we [Ruthie and Jedidjah] got close.

Q: Tell me about Jonathan. As a child, I would think that you saw the effort your parents made to help him realize his potential. How did this affect you at the time?

A: It didn't bother me in the least. I was the one that was baby-sitting when he was born. I didn't know he had Down syndrome. It wouldn't matter with me anyway. She [Carla] very much treated him as an only child and excluded us. He got 100 percent attention. They were always looking for a religious place for him to live. They didn't want the religion just thrown behind. She wanted to concentrate on doing the best for him. She couldn't split herself and share.

**

Ruthie Goldstein

Ruthie was the first child of Carla and Bernie. She is a strong, vibrant Orthodox woman, equally devoted to her family, profession, and faith. A photo of Ruthie sits on Carla's buffet. It shows a religious woman with a warm, loving smile. Her brown eyes are calm. She has Bernie's cheeks. Her complexion is dark. I would bet she was Israeli, not Dutch. For the first year or so, I thought her name was "Ru-tee" because of Carla's accent. It was not until the early fall of 2003, when Carla went to visit Ruthie in New York and wrote down her phone number for "just in case" purposes, that I realized her real name. While visiting Ruthie, during Sukkot, Carla took a hard fall going down the cement steps of Ruthie's door leading to the backyard. Her shoulder was broken, and her leg was so badly bruised that there was serious concern about clotting.

What started out as a week of being with the family for the festival of Sukkot turned into a serious hospital stay and slow convalescence in New York. Although I have briefly met Ruthie while she visited with her parents in Jacksonville, our interview took place via the phone.

Q: Tell me how your parents' hiding influenced your upbringing?

A: It didn't affect it much. They really didn't talk about it. It is coming out in the later years. It was never discussed in my house. I left Holland too young to really remember too much because I was born after the war.

Q: How do your parents influence your life today?

A: I look at my parents and where they come from and what they have been through. It is quite amazing and unbelievable. Added to that is Jonathan. They are an inspiration. They have survived and are together, even though we are separated by distance.

Q: Were the events of World War II ever discussed between your parents or your siblings?

A: I don't think we did. They [Channa and Jedidjah] have much more involvement. I am closer to my sister in Israel. We are sisters, although we are half sisters. It was a whole family. It was never a difference and very special. Growing up, we were all one.

Q: How do you handle Jonathan and his needs with your family? You obviously live closest.

A: My children are aware of Uncle Jon and the fact that he has disabilities. It has never been a problem. It is more a problem to me now. I am trying to see that my children marry, but it is a cruel world... *shidduch*-wise, my son... the [Jonathan's]Down syndrome...

Q: Do your children know about your parents' hiding?

A: The children know about their grandparents' experience. It is fascinating to them. It is only within the past ten years that she [Carla] has shared. Maybe when they are getting older and thinking, at this point... you feel your mortality. Maybe they feel more comfortable. That is not so much as a hurt, but they can talk about it.

Q: Did you know they were survivors when you were a child?

A: I knew about it as a child because I knew my sisters had a different father. It was something that had happened, but we never discussed it. Never.

Q: Carla's upbringing as a child had a certain distance and formality. Did you experience anything similar?

A: Yes, they were reserved, but they [Carla's parents] weren't young when they had her.

Q: I realize that you were young when your family left Holland. Do you have any early memories?

A: I remember in Holland that I had to go upstairs to our apartment, and I had to ring the bell, and I couldn't reach it. My mother tells me that I was the meatball.

Q: What are some of your memories of moving and living in New York?

A: I remember Aunt Rose and the daughters not being very nice to me. Gee, it must have been hard for her, too. She treated us as a burden. She gave us rye bread with seeds in it; and as a child, I didn't like that, but she didn't care. I remember that I went to Moshava, a day camp in Montreal, Canada.

Q: Did you have many friends?

A: I had one or two close friends growing up. And I am still friendly with those. I never needed lots.

Q: Describe Jonathan's influence on your family life.

A: I was like nine or ten when he was born. I didn't realize that something was the matter. To me, he was my little brother. Only, later on, he didn't progress as quickly as others. We took care of him because my mother had to work. We had to take over. My parents were always pushing to have things done with him. My sisters think that I got left out and had to grow up by myself because Jonathan was the focus. I don't think so because I am an individualistic person and always can find something to do. They were the caretakers.

Q: Your mother studied nursing, and you are an accomplished nurse. Describe your training.

A: I always wanted to be a nurse from day one. I went to public school until sixth grade in Washington Heights. Then, I went to Yeshiva Rabbi Samson Raphael Hirsch in Washington Heights. I went from public school and Talmud Torah to yeshiva. The transition was difficult. I played catch-up with a tutor. From ages seven to eleven, I was at the yeshiva. I realized it was costing my parents a lot of money, so I decided to leave and went to George Washington Heights High School and graduated in January 1965. I wanted to go to Hunter, so I went at night for six months. Then, I went to a three-year nursing program at New Rochelle Hospital School of Nursing, graduating in 1969.

Then, when we lived in Washington Heights, my dream was to work at Columbia Presbyterian. I worked there in the operating room. My family said that I was full of operating-room stories. They had excellent training, but they gave me a problem about Shabbos. I worked on Shabbos for a year and a half, and it didn't sit well with me. I walked to work. I did the least I could. I decided I was going to leave. They offered me the position of teaching the technicians. It was prestigious, but I wasn't ready for that. So I started working in the Bronx at Albert Einstein Hospital. I met the supervisor who was married to a Jew, and she respected my wishes because I told her that the one thing I won't do is abortions. I was there from 1971 to 1982. When I left there, I was teaching operating-room nursing. I spent one year at Long Island Jewish Hospital in a management position, but I hated it. It was a bad time in my family life, and the atmosphere was cliquey. I quit and I didn't go back to work until Albert Einstein in February 1985 part-time. I am a staff nurse and the team leader.

Q: You are an Orthodox Jew, like your parents. Discuss your Judaism.

A: My parents definitely influenced that. We are Orthodox Jewish. We haven't gone very, very right wing. We may be a little more Orthodox than my parents because of the schooling. I think from when my husband and I married that once we retire, we plan to make aliyah. My son is waiting for us to come. I am getting ready to retire. Maybe a five-year plan or a little less. I can retire in three years. The problem is Jonathan. If there is something in Israel maybe, and they could take good care of him. It is kind of an unknown. I am sure he would love it, but he's not getting any younger.

Q: Do you think Jonathan has any idea about your parents' history?

A: I think Jonathan is very into his own world.

Q: Your mother's devotion to Hashem permeates her life. She believes that there are no coincidences. Even though she suffered greatly during World War II, she never doubted her belief in God. Is this a trait of your mother's or a universal Orthodox belief?

A: This is an Orthodox thought. A lot of people think this way in the back of their minds. The more Orthodox, the more this devotion is a living part of their life. You never look back and feel sorry.

From Snow to Sand

Carla recently told me about a dream. "I was walking from Zwolle to Marle, but it was not snow but sand." In the dream, she was cold, miserable, depressed. She was frightened and numb. She spars with her saga of hiding on a daily and nightly basis. Her constant intestinal and digestive struggles have her tethered to the closest bathroom. Our discussions exhaust her body, heart, and mind. Even Carla's dreams cannot escape. How can we ever imagine the walk that each survivor has made?

During a conversation with Bernie about how he and his brother dealt with the nerve-wracking hours, weeks, months, and seasons of hiding, he excused himself and went to his study. After a few minutes, he reappeared with a small worn red German and English dictionary. Although yellowed from time, the inside of the book is in excellent condition. A handwritten key is meticulously penciled inside the front cover. The key is a listing of notations including dashes, marks, asterisks, and the corresponding meaning for each of these entries. Throughout the book, written in fine penmanship, before each word entry, Henry inserted the appropriate notation to help the brothers master their grasp of English. His symbols included small squares, dashes, and phonetic English and German words, *carefully printed. By exercising their minds, they survived, one word at a time.*

I constantly admire Carla's bookshelves. It is not the wealth of Jewish knowledge that the books contain that impresses me. The shelves are bowed also with family photographs. Little kids with big blue eyes smile. Wedding photos with hordes of hugging cousins adorn the shelves. The standard school snapshots and old Polaroids in yellowing Lucite frames all display a proud Jewish history. Despite the Nazis' attempt to annihilate the Jews from the world, they flourish.

Carla and Bernie have an ancient prayer book. The pages are browned, flaking away. Family members' names are meticulously written in Dutch, English, and Hebrew. Births, marriages, and deaths are all recorded inside the front cover. Names are written in Hebrew, Dutch, and English. The "Who's Who" of Carla's and Bernie's family can be found in this quiet, humble place. Carla calls off the roll: Ruthie and Yankee became parents in 1976 to Joseph, 1981 with Gedalyahu Elizer, and D. Yizak in 1983. Channa and Leon had Andre in 1977, and Julian in 1980. Jedidjah and Michah had Tanya in 1966, Ashi in 1968. Rina Aterah in 1976. Margalith Niza was born in 1977, and then Amichai Yehoshua was born in 1981. Tanya married to David Greenberg in 1987. Presently, they live in Malei Adumim and are raising five girls: Ayala Sorah, born in 1991; Na'ama, born in 1992; Tehilla, born in 1994; Reut Chavah, born in 1997; Tiferet, born in 2002. Asher, named after Andre, married Esther Shanie Miller. They are raising five children: Jacob, born in 1994; Tzivyah, born in 1996; Yehudah, born in 1998; Raya Sarah, named after Ruth, Bernie's mother, born in 2001. Margalith was married to Yoram Silverman in 1997. They have Adereth, born in 1998; Shalhevet, born in 2000; Shira, born in 2002; and Natanel Yosef, born in 2004. Atarah just married Yuval Regev. Presently, Carla and Bernie have ten grandchildren and fourteen great-grandchildren, a testament to Carla's determined spirit.

**

Jonathan's independence finally gave Carla and Bernie a chance to determine their retirement years. "We were on our own in New Rochelle, three flights up in a garden apartment. It became too much." Carla and Bernie decided that they did not need to live in New Rochelle any longer. "When Jonathan was okay, we didn't need to be there." Independent like her father, Carla and Bernie explored the opportunity of moving to Jacksonville, Florida.

Near our apartment on Wadsworth Avenue, I was buying some things in a grocery store for Pesach in 1956. I met the owner and his wife, Joseph and Herta Verstandig. I felt a connection right away. They are both Holocaust survivors. She and I became very close. We were in Jacksonville in June 1993 for Herta's granddaughter's wedding. We had a good time. Herta asked me if I knew that they were going to build some small houses like a community there. My idea was that I didn't want to become a burden to my children. With our age, we were having some problems with the winter. That February, back in New York, Herta Verstandig and Yosef said that they were going to build The Coves, a retirement community south of Jacksonville. I said, "I want to be in it." And my husband, who never makes up his mind about anything, says, "Yeah, okay." They started building in January of 1994, and we moved on January 3, 1995. We left New York during a snowstorm. It was seventeen degrees.

Carla and Bernie were some of the first residents to move into The Coves. Carla's vast network of friends keep in touch with overnight visits, a constant stream of telephone calls and emails. "You know, I'll be thinking, 'I've got to call Carla,' and the phone will ring, and it's her," says Paul Rosenfeld, who now is an assistant state attorney in the Bronx. "Carla and Bernie are so *haimish*, such good people. I never knew their story. I think maybe she hid during the war? Here are two good people who had some horrible things happen to them, and they have accomplished so much. I admire their faith. They have good *neshama*, good souls.

You know, she leaves you with a warm feeling that doesn't go away."

Today, Carla speaks to her childhood friend Leida approximately once a month. She and Tetta speak less frequently. "About sixteen years ago, we all got together in Switzerland. Leida arranged things from Holland. We had a good time. We rented some rooms in a house. The bathroom was located across the balcony. I didn't like that. It reminded me of the war. I enjoyed the trip in a way, but the accommodations had put a big damper on me."

Through phone calls, letters, e-mails, and photos, Carla has kept her friendships nestled closely around her heart. She still keeps in touch with Inge Adler, the Greenbergs, Paul Rosenfeld, Renee Hirsch, Bezazel Shandelman, and Louis Franken, a relation to Andre's Tanta Ro. "He is like another son to us." Her vast collection of admiring friends is, like her family, a prized possession. "I am an only child, so I know how important it is to have friends."

**

In March 2005, Carla hands me a card. It is on ivory paper and yellowing around the edges. On the front is a pen and ink sketch of their home at the Coves. I open it. Stamped on the left side is a New Address announcement with their present Jacksonville street and phone number. The message on the other side reads:

> Friends are like precious jewels. Each is unique, with interesting facets and sparkling brilliance. Minor flaws are overshadowed by superior character and quality. Each is priceless and irreplaceable. We believe friends are chosen because they fulfill a need or possess a trait to which we aspire. Some are blessed with a great sense of humor; some have compassion or never-ending patience. We have friends whose advice we trust, friends whose talents we envy and friends who,

after all these years, never cease to amaze us. All our friends have their own personality, and within each group, we have our own special niche. All our friends are like precious jewels, and we are surely very blessed in having such a treasure. Thank you for making us wealthy with the gift of your friendship.

"I found some of this, but I added my own thoughts to it and made it mine," she explains. "Keep it."
I slip the card in my bag.
Another gift.

Acknowledgments

When I became pregnant with my first child, I began to ignore any subject matter about the Holocaust. It was an easy shift to make. I had had my fill of Holocaust history, frustration, disgust, and disbelief. With a new life being nurtured within me, I saw my new abhorrence to this "human tragedy" as my first protective maternal instinct. Because I could not mentally grapple with the catastrophic pain of such an event, I somehow concocted a "hall pass" mentality. I make no apologies for this thought process. For twelve years, I managed to wear beautifully this blindfold.

Approximately four and a half months into my second pregnancy, after a routine sonogram, I was told there may be something wrong with my child's brain. Genetic testing revealed that my child was a candidate for a litany of neurological issues, including Down syndrome. High-risk doctors, genetic counselors, obstetric nurses, and mournful anger filled my pregnancy. Further, extensive testing finally negated these assumptions. I swore I would never get pregnant again, opting, yet a second time, for the hall pass.

It is no accident that I reluctantly met Carla Schipper.

It was Gail Greenfield, a cousin of my husband's and a nurse at Camp Ramah Palmer, who introduced us.

Now, I have full appreciation for the concept of bashert. In the span of mankind's history, Carla's story is not horrible. Painful to hear? Perhaps. Uncomfortable to read? Maybe. In the end it is, simply put, the true account of her life, as seen through her, her family, and friends, now permanently archived on paper—for no one to deny.

This documentation would not have been possible if Carla, Bernie, Channa, Jedidjah, Ruthie, and Jonathan did not agree to speak candidly and truthfully. I am greatly indebted to them for their trust in this endeavor.

I have an incalculable respect for each of these individuals. Their personal stories are precious testimonials to the collective history of this era.

Gratitude is deeply extended to Sidney Sherter, PhD, professor of history, emeritus, Long Island University, New York. His passionate dedication to preserving and honoring the memory of the six million murdered Jews was a relentless motivation.

My priceless book group: Meryl Rittenberg, my gatherer of an overwhelming network of knowledge, talent, and support; Ellen Kopp, an exquisite editor par excellence; Doris Goldstein, a fellow former journalist, whose judgments were always correct; Claudia Baker, Iris Kraemer, Marla Lewis, Randi Rogozinski, Lisa Wolfson, and Arlene Yegelwel are all brilliant friends and ruthlessly objective book critics. This powerful minyan served as my literary gold standard, constantly providing me with inspiration, known and unbeknownst to each of them.

Leslie Frilling, John Iorii, Terry Nelson and Jeanine Rogozinski each tendered reliable advice, opinion and direction that forced my writing to constantly respect the reader.

Having a cuppa and scones with Elizabeth Marx has been a ceaseless motivation in bringing this book to print. Once bound, I'm on my way back to Brisbane for a long afternoon at the Sherwood Arboretum.

Without the gifted artist, Renee Berg, who also served as my solid sounding board, the cover would still be buried deep inside my head. Only a sister could extract it with such precision and panache.

I thank my sons, Bradley and Jeffrey, who gave me endless unsolicited support, even when they had no clean clothes (not that they cared about that), an empty fridge, and an occasional forgotten lunch. All threats of "What if I delete this?" and "Are you ever going to be done?" were always understood within context.

It was a freezing, cloudy, gray, windy day in February 2004 when I knocked on an author's door. A nervous wreck, the cold salty ocean wind whipping my hair across my face, I stood in front of the door, holding a small frail orchid and a huge case of writer's block.

Over a cup of tea, the author simply told me to find my own voice and "just write."

It was as if I had drunk a gallon of tea and could not get to the bathroom fast enough. The words began to spew out. Not flow, mind you, but erupt. Sometimes, I could not keep track of them. Sometimes the words were, frankly, not so hot.

But the words were there. And any writer is thankful for that.

I am eternally grateful for that calming conversion and the warm cup of tea.

It was the hall pass I could face.

Finally, I have the greatest respect and love for my husband, Bruce, who knew from the start that this was my own flight.

Notes

All the information in the chronological tables throughout *On Wooden Wheels* was compiled based on data and history from excellent sources listed in the bibliography. Because such a vast amount of information exists, in both English, Dutch and Hebrew, regarding the subject matter, I have tried to be as accurate as possible, understanding that occasionally data may conflict regarding a date, number or spelling.

January 2005

[1] Cunningham, *Understanding Down syndrome: an Introduction for Parents*, 88, 105.
[2] Leshin, "Trisomy 21: The Story of Down Syndrome," 1
[3] Cunningham, 155.
[4] Ibid., 107.

Solitary Musings

[5] Victor, "Netherlands." Judaica Philatelic Resources. *http://www.edwardvictor/NetherlandsFrame2main.htm*
[6] Dwork and van Pelt, "The Netherlands," in *The World Reacts to the Holocaust*. Edited by David S. Wyman, 45-46.

[7] Victor, "Netherlands." Judaica Philatelic Resources. http://www.edwardvictor/NetherlandsFrame2main.htm
[8] Dwork and van Pelt, 47.
[9] Victor, 1.
[10] Dwork and van Pelt, 47-49.
[11] Yahil, *The Holocaust: The Fate of European Jewry*, 226.
[12] Dwork and van Pelt, 50.
[13] Edelheit, *History of the Holocaust: a Handbook and Dictionary*, 206.
[14] Laqueur, Walter, ed. *The Holocaust Encyclopedia*," xxii.
[15] Edelheit, 206.
[16] Laqueur, xxii.

Andre Andriesse

[17] Dwork and van Pelt, 51-52.
[18] Laqueur, xxiii-xxiv.
[19] Ibid., xxiv-vi.
[20] Fogelman, "The Rescuer Self," 664.
[21] Ibid., xxvi.
[22] de Jong, *The Netherlands and Nazi Germany*, 8-9. And www.ushmm.org/wlc/article.php?lang=en&ModuleId=10 005436.
[23] Yahil, *The Holocaust: The Fate of European Jewry*, 338-339.
[24] www.ushmm.org/wlc/article.php?lang=en&ModuleId=10 005436.
[25] de Jong, 11.
[26] Bauer, *A History of the Holocaust*, 240-243.
[27] Ibid.
[28] Yahil, *The Holocaust: The Fate of European Jewry*, 337.
[29] Ibid.
[30] Bauer, 240-24.

Not the Only One

[31] Ibid., 240-243.
[32] de Jong, 12-13.
[33] Bauer, 240-243.
[34] Yahil, *The Holocaust: The Fate of European Jewry*, 392.
[35] Ibid., 391.

[36] de Jong, 14.
[37] Yahil, *The Holocaust: The Fate of European Jewry*, 393.

Go Back to Bed

[38] Tec, "Reflections on Rescuers," In *The Holocaust and History, The Known, the Unknown, the Disputed and the Reexamined.* Edited by Michael Berenbaum and Abraham J. Peck, 558, 660.
[39] Ibid., 664.
[40] de Jong, 21.
[41] Tec, 656.
[42] Yahil, 338.
[43] de Jong 10,16-17, 34.

The Offer

[44] Yahil, *The Holocaust: The Fate of European Jewry*, 439.

Collecting Fragments

[45] de Jong, 35.
[46] Yahil, *The Holocaust: The Fate of European Jewry*, 439-440.
[47] http//www.edwardvictor.com/NetherlandsFrame2main.htm.
[48] *www.joodscheraadenschede.nl/Onderwerpen/verzet/226.htm*
Dutch language sources were translated by Carla and Bernie Schipper. Often, these translative sessions included several etymological sources.
[49] Cunningham, 152.

Laying a Foundation

[50] Wilson, Michael, "Rudolf Steiner".

Finding His Place

[51] Leshin, 3.

Glossary

Dutch, English, Hebrew, and Yiddish. All these languages figure into Carla's vast lexicon. The glossary below will help grasp the nuances of her story.

E = English   H = Hebrew   Y = Yiddish

Agudas or **Agudat Yisrael** (H). "Society of Israel," a political, communal, and cultural voice of Orthodox Jews, although not all members were Orthodox Jews. Founded in 1912. *Agudah* meaning "together" or "union." *Yisrael* meaning "Israel."

aliyah (H). Ascending. For Jews, it is the act of relocating from anywhere to Israel. Carla's daughter, Jedidjah Gross, made *aliyah* from the United States to Israel.

aveilous or **ovel** (Y). A period of mourning lasting one year. During Carla's and Andre's wedding reception, no music or dancing occured out of respect for Carla's mourning period, *aveilous*.

bar mitzvah. Ceremony for a Jewish boy, thirteen years old, that signifies he has accepted the responsibilities associated with being a Jewish adult. Blessings, reading from the Torah and the Book of Prophets are components of this rite of passage.

bashert (Y). God's will; meant to happen.

bensch (Y). Praying after meals.

B'nai Akivah (H). Orthodox Jewish youth group.

brochot (H). Blessings; the singular is *bracha*.

cantor (E). See *hazzan*.

chesed (H). Kindness.

chuppah (H). Jewish wedding canopy; it represents the home that the couple will build together.

daven/davening (Y). Pray or praying.

De Joodsche Raad (D). The Jewish Council. In Holland, a group of Jewish leaders organized by the Nazis to collect information on the Jewish population. The council was an important tool in organizing the mass deportations to the concentration camps. These councils were set up in many of the Nazi-occupied countries.

dominee (D). Minister.

erythema nodosum or *erythemanodosum* (E). Eruptions of red tender bumps of the legs below the knees or shins, of pink to blue tender nodules appearing in crops, more frequently seen in women, and often associated with joint pains, fever, and enlarged lymph nodes. It is usually associated with another ailment. Most likely, in Carla's case, these were perhaps ulcers, colitis, or irritable bowel syndrome. It can also be a reaction to a medication. While treated by a kind doctor in Marle, she may have received medication that could have been contaminated.

frum (Y). Very religious; observant of religious laws and customs.

Gemara (H). Rabbinical commentaries and analysis on the Mishnah. These two components comprise the Talmud, a compilation of rabbinic commentary on all aspects of Jewish life, including Jewish law, customs, ethics, and moral issues.

gehucht (D). Small area with just a few farms.

Green Cross. Medical corps program in Holland.
Goyish (Y). Non-Jewish.
hachsharah (H). Literally means "preparation." Hachsharahs or hachsharim were Orthodox Zionist agricultural communities where young Jewish individuals lived. They learned farming and other skills that would prepare them for life in Israel.
hachnosas orchim (H). The good deed of inviting a traveler into your home.
haftarah (H). Reading from the prophets that has a similar theme or message of the Torah portion. It is read after the Torah portion is completed; special blessings are sung before and after the reading. The haftarah is recited with specific cantillation or trop.
hazzan or ***chazzan*** (H). The cantorial leader of a congregation, responsible for setting the melody, tone and emotion.
haart (D). Decorative hearth.
heimish (Y). Good-natured, kind individual.
Holocaust (E). Term for Nazi Germany's mass annihilation of six million Jews during the Second World War. Nazi Germany, led by Adolf Hitler, referred to this genocide as the "Final Solution." The label "Holocaust" is from the Greek, *holokauston*, meaning sacrificial whole offering consumed by fire. Some scholars refute this label, arguing that there exists no sacrificial significance and no relation to fire. Many scholars include the five million other persecuted minorities in the Holocaust victim roll. These include gypsies, homosexuals, intellectuals, sympathizers, Catholics, Slavs, disabled, and political dissidents. Presently, the term "holocaust" is found in media and published works, referring to mass killings that are unfortunately still happening as of this writing. See *Shoah*.
Hongerwinter. (D). Hunger winter. The famine that overtook the Netherlands from October 1944 to May 1945 due to the Nazi blockade of food and necessary materials.

imker (D). Beekeeper.
Kohaynim (H). Kohayn is a priest. This is the plural form. Kohaynim are direct male descendants of Biblical Aaron. The Kohaynim hold a distinct status in Judaism.
layning/lyning (Y). Reading the Torah with the proper pronunciation and melodic intonations and inflections.
lilliput (D). Small person.
mazel (Y). Luck.
minyan (H). Ten men; the minimum required to conduct a service.
mitzvah or ***mitzvoth*** (H). Commandment.
mohel (Y). Individual who performs the brit milah, ritual circumcision for males entering the Jewish faith.
mensch (Y). A male who acts in a truly respectable manner.
ORT (H). An international charitable organization network that offers education, training schools, colleges, and training centers in order to aid in the advancement of the Jewish people. The acronym is derived from the original Russian name.
parsha or ***parshas*** (H). A portion of the Torah.
Pesach (H). The Jewish holiday of Passover, celebrating the exodus from Egypt. Passover is celebrated for eight days. In the United States, the first two days include a Seder, a ceremonial meal with symbols retelling the exodus story.
Poale Mizrahi, Ha Poale Yisrael, Poale Agudath Yisrael, PIA (H). Orthodox Jewish Zionist *hachsharahs/hachsharim*. These groups offered housing and necessary agricultural skills to religious Jews that planned to move to Israel before and after the war. These organizations were part of the ***Agudas*** or ***Agudat Yisrael*** communal, and cultural voice of Orthodox Jews, although not all members were Orthodox Jews. Founded in 1912. *Agudah* means "together" or "union." *Yisrael* is Hebrew for "Israel." This group existed in contrast to the non- religious Zionist movement pioneered by Theodor Herzl. Carla's father was against the Zionist movement.

pleurisy (E). Inflammation of the lung tissue.
razzia (D). Roundup or mass arrest of Jews in Holland by the Nazis; first step in deportation to extermination.
Rosh Hashanah (H). Jewish New Year.
Rosh Chodesh (H). *Rosh*, meaning "head"; *Hodesh*, meaning "month."
Rosh Pina (H). Cornerstone.
Seder (H). Order; service leading to Passover.
Sefer Torah (H). The Torah; the first five books of the Bible.
selichot (H). Prayers asking for forgiveness that are offered eight to ten days before *Rosh Hashanah*.
shiorim (H). Lectures.
Shabbat or ***Shabbos*** (H). Jewish Sabbath, from sundown Friday night to sundown Saturday night.
shacharit (H). Morning prayers recited every weekday morning.
Shalaym (H). Complete; organization that formed with the Tikvah parents. Carla was its president.
shammes (Y). An individual who assists in the synagogue.
shaytl (Y). Wig worn by Orthodox Jewish women.
shickered (Y). Drunk.
shiva (H). The seven days of morning following the burial of a loved one.
shoah (H). Complete annihilation of the Jewish people. A biblical term meaning "unforeseen disaster." In the United States, the accepted term is also "Holocaust." Much debate surrounds the appropriate terminology for such a horrendous human tragedy. Shoah is the preferred term in Israel. See Holocaust.
shochet (Y). Ritual slaughterer. Philip de Groot, Carla's friend in Enschede, was a shochet.
shmooze (Y). To network, chat, and converse.
shul (Y). Synagogue.
Sukkot (H). Jewish holiday, one of three categorized as festivals. Sukkot commemorates the Israelites' life in the desert on their pilgrimage to the Land of Israel. Sukkot is

celebrated on the Hebrew calendar on the fifteenth day of the Hebrew month of Tishrei. For most Jews, the festive holiday lasts for eight days and includes building a booth or sukkah to resemble living under the heavens in the desert. Symbols of the desert experience include the lulav, an assortment of willow and myrtle branches, and an etrog, a lemon-like fruit.

Talmud Torah (H). Hebrew school.

Talmud (H). Thoroughly written compilation of rabbinic commentary on Jewish law, ethics, morals, customs, and all aspects of Jewish life.

tefillin (H). Or phylacteries; prayers written on kosher parchment enclosed in small square boxes. Each box is attached with leather straps. One set is worn on the forehead and another around the arm. These are worn during morning prayers as a reminder to the heart, hand and head of Hashem's commandments.

teno'im (H). Engagement ceremony.

tikun olam (H). The act of repairing the world; generosity; kindness; philanthropy.

tikvah (H). Hope.

verpleegster (D). Certified nurse.

verraad (D). Betrayal.

WIZO (E). Women's International Zionist Organization; philanthropic organization that supports Israel.

Yad Vashem (H). Yad Vashem, The Holocaust Martyrs' and Heroes' Remembrance Authority is Israel's official memorial to the Jewish victims of the Holocaust, located in Jerusalem. Established in 1953. In Hebrew, "a memorial and a name." The origin of the name is from the Biblical verse Isaiah 56:5: "And to them I will give in my house and within my walls a memorial and a name." Yad Vashem includes a museum, memorials to the victims including children, an educational center, art gallery, archive and a memorial to the "Righteous Among Nations," non-Jews who risked their lives in an effort to save Jews.

yeshiva (H). A school or academy that focuses on intense Torah studies.

Yuntov (Y). Derived from the Hebrew words *yom*, meaning "day," and *tov*, meaning "good"; holiday.

zaftig (Y). Description of an individual who is pudgy or a bit overweight.

Zionism (E). Established in 1897 by Theodor Herzl. A belief and conviction that Jews must forge their own destiny as a nation with a Jewish homeland. The Zionist movement is responsible for organizing and implementing the first colonies in Palestine and creating the state of Israel after World War II. The Zionist movement is not a religious movement. Many Orthodox Jews were anti-Zionists, believing that only with the coming of the Messiah would Israel become a Jewish homeland.

Bibliography

Bauer, Yehuda. *A History of the Holocaust.* New York: Franklin Watts, 1982.

Beem, H. *Joden van Leeuwarden: Geshiedenis van een Jods Cultuurcentum.* Van Gorcum and Comp. B.B.: Assen, 1974.

Cunningham, Cliff. *Understanding Down Syndrome: an Introduction for Parents.* Cambridge: Brookline Books, 1996.

"Ds. Leendert Overduin," De Joodsche Raad in Enschede (Enschede Jewish Council), *http://joodscheraadenschede.nl/Onderwerpen/verzet/226/htm*

Dwork, Deborah, and Pelt. "The Netherlands." In *The World Reacts to the Holocaust.* Edited by David S. Wyman. Baltimore: Johns Hopkins University Press, 1996.

Edelheit, Abraham J., and Hershel Edelheit. *History of the Holocaust: a Handbook and Dictionary.* Boulder: Westview Press, 1994.

Fogelman, Eva. "The Rescuer Self." In *The Holocaust and History, The Known, the Unknown, the Disputed and the Reexamined.* Edited by Michael Berenbaum and Abraham J. Peck. Bloomington: Indiana University Press, 1998.

Greenberg, Herb and Greenberg. E-mail correspondence that included "The Tikvah Program at Camp Ramah in New England," paper delivered at the Second Annual International Conference on Jewish Special Education, Tel Aviv University. Tel Aviv, Israel, 1993.

Iorii, John, Holocaust scholar and educator, Jacksonville, Florida, in discussion with the author. September 2004.

Jong, Louis de. *The Netherlands and Nazi Germany*. Cambridge: Harvard University Press, 1990.

Laqueur, Walter. ed. *The Holocaust Encyclopedia*. New Haven: Yale University Press, 2000.

Leshin, Les, MD, FAAP. "Trisomy 21: The Story of Down Syndrome." Down Syndrome: Health Issues. http: // www.ds-health.com/trisomy.htm

Wilson, Michael. Excerpt from "Rudolf Steiner, From the introduction *to The Philosophy of Freedom*." Rudolf Steiner Archive *http://www.rsarchive. org/RSBio.php*

Victor, Edward. "Netherlands." Judaica Philatelic Resources. *http://www. edwardvictor.com/NetherlandsFrame2main.htm*

Tec, Nachama. "Reflections on Rescuers," In *The Holocaust and History, The Known, the Unknown, the Disputed and the Reexamined*. Edited by Michael Berenbaum and Abraham J. Peck. Bloomington: Indiana University Press, 1998.

Yahil, Leni. *The Holocaust: The Fate of European Jewry, 1932-1945*. New York: Oxford, 1987.

Further Reading

Berger, Alan and Gloria Cronin, editors. *Jewish American and Holocaust Literature: Representation in the Postmodern World* (SUNY Press, September 2004).

Berenbaum. Michael, editor. *The Holocaust and History: The Known, the Unknown, the Disputed and the Reexamined* (Bloomington: Indiana University Press, 2002).

Boas, Jacob. *Boulevard des Miseres: The Story of Transit Camp Westerbork* (Hamden, CT: Anchor Books, 1985).

de Jong, Louis. *Het Koninkrijk der Nederlanden in de Tweede Wereldoorlog* (Den Haag: SDU Uitgeverij Koninginnegracht, 12 volumes, 1969-1988).

Dwork, Deborah. *Children with a Star: Jewish Youth in Nazi Europe* (New Haven: Yale University Press, 1991).

Gilbert, Martin. *The Holocaust: A History of the Jews During the Second World War* (New York: Holt Rinehart and Winston, 1985).

Hilberg, Raul. *The Destruction of the European Jews* (New Haven: Yale University Press, 3 Volumes, 2003).

Langer, Lawrence. *Holocaust Testimonies: The Ruins of Memory* (New Haven and London: Yale University Press, 1991).

Levi, Primo. *The Drowned and the Saved* (New York, Vintage, 1989) and *Survival in Auschwitz: The Nazi Assault on Humanity* (New York: Touchstone; Reprint edition, 1995).

Marrus Michael, *The Holocaust in History* (Hanover and London: Brandeis University Press, 1987).

Tec, Nechama. *Dry Tears* (Oxford University Press, 1982) and *When Light Pierced the Darkness*, (Oxford University Press, 1986).

Wiesenthal, Simon. *The Sunflower* (Schocken Books, 1976).

Wyman, David S. *The Abandonment of the Jews: America and the Holocaust, 1941-1945* (New York: The New Press 1998).

Made in the USA
Lexington, KY
15 October 2013